HEROES
OF THE BIRMINGHAM
AIR RAIDS

HEROES
OF THE BIRMINGHAM
AIR RAIDS

A TRIBUTE TO BIRMINGHAM'S
HEROES 1940 - 1943 WITH DETAILS
OF MEDALS AWARDED

by

MICHAEL MINTON

BREWIN BOOKS

First published by
Brewin Books Ltd, 56 Alcester Road,
Studley, Warwickshire B80 7LG in 2002
www.brewinbooks.com

ISBN 1 85858 211 3

A Cataloguing in Publication Record
for this title is available from the British Library.

Typeset in Times
Printed in Great Britain by
Warwick Printing Company Limited.

This is not a history of the Birmingham Blitz but a record of the gallant deeds performed, in most cases by the citizens of Birmingham. During very troubled and difficult times Birmingham, which was described as "A town in the West Midlands", suffered a great many casualties including over 2,200 killed and many more injured. At the same time one third of the city's houses were damaged or destroyed. No record of bravery or heroism of this era can ever be complete, for medals or recognition went only to a few. To the many who also served without recognition, we that remain, remember you and are for ever indebted to you.

Michael Minton

Acknowledgements

4th Battalion Home Guard
  (1948 Private Collection)
29th Battalion Home Guard,
  Birmingham 1948
47th Warwickshire Battalion
  March 1944
Animal World
Birmingham City Archives
Birmingham Central Library
  Local Studies and History Service
Birmingham Evening Despatch
Birmingham Evening Mail
Birmingham Gazette
Birmingham Mail
Birmingham Museum & Art Gallery
Birmingham Post & Mail
Gas Department (George Medalists)
Heroes of Road and Rail
  by George Churnock. Pub. 1941

History of Home Guard Battalions
Home Guard List, Western Command
Imperial War Museum
London Gazette
Minton Collection
O.M.R.S. re Calypso Gammon
Sunday Mercury

Thanks to

Chris Shelley for his time and effort in editing the book. To Patrick Baird of Birmingham Libraries for his invaluable help. To Dr. Lloyd, June & Peter Done, Tony Sabell, my family and members of the Birmingham Medal Society for their support and encouragement to enable me to get my brother's work published. – *Margaret Fisher*

Medal Descriptions from the frontispiece - (From left to right)

Top Row: Life Saving Medal of the order of St. John, B.E.M. - British Empire Medal, Military Medal, Fire Brigade Medal - Assoc. of Professional Fire Brigade Officers for Long Service.
Middle Row: R.S.P.C.A. Bronze Medal, R.S.P.C.A. Margaret Wheatley Cross, Fire Brigade Medal for Conspicuous Bravery, O.B.E. - Order of British Empire Medal,
Bottom Row: Fire Brigade Medal for Long Service, R.S.P.C.A. Silver Medal for Humanity Animal Life Saving, Police Medal - Obverse, Police Medal - Reverse.

Insignia Descriptions from the previous page - (From left to right)

Top Row: Women's Land Army, ARP,
Civil Nursing Reserve, WVS, Civil Defence.
Bottom Row: Birmingham's Home Defence Corps, Co-op ARP,
Teachers' Evacuation Hostel Badge, Factory ARP.

About The Author
- Michael Francis Minton

Mike Minton who died suddenly at his home on Monday 20th December 1993, was born in the Selly Park district of Birmingham on 25th January 1937, The son of Francis and Violet Minton. He attended schools in Selly Park and Bournbrook and completed his education at Bournville College.

In 1954 he began his National Service with the Royal Warwickshire Regiment, with which he felt some family connection, since his grandfather has been RSM during the First World War period. This factor was to have considerable influence on his medal collecting. For most of his National Service he served on the Headquarters Staff of Northern Command at York and during this time he developed a keen interest in pot-holing, a pastime which he continued for some time after leaving the army.

Mike Minton's career was spent largely on the staff of Messrs. Dun & Bradstreet Ltd. in Birmingham, a firm engaged in credit investigations. It may be that this style of work was consistent with his unceasing research work into medal-related personalities. These medal interests began around the time of his National Service and persisted throughout his life. His membership of the Orders and Medals Research Society started in 1964 with a membership of 540.

Michael was one of the founder members of the Birmingham Medal Society, which was inaugurated in 1964 at a meeting held in the premises of Forman's Medals, then in Summer Row, Birmingham. He became secretary of the society and its President from 1970 to 1979. His service on the committee of the Birmingham Society had been continuous from 1964 until his death.

Apart from his obvious commitment to the 6th Foot/Royal Warwickshire Regt. and the Warwickshire Yeomanry, Michael had several other specialist themes. These included for example, medals related to animals, gallantry, life saving, and the RSPCA. He had always shown a great fondness for animals and had been a dog owner for many years. During his last few years he had formed a considerable liking for ferrets, an interest shared by several members of the Birmingham Society.

Mike Minton had extensively researched the Birmingham and Coventry Blitz, and had a great knowledge of the Birmingham Home Guard and bomb disposal work within the area. He became an authority on the George Medal and other gallantry awards to Midlanders, for this period. He also had close contacts with the Birmingham Police Museum as well as with the Birmingham Fire Brigade, both organisations having played an important role in the Second World War. His spare time during lunch hours was often spent in the local studies department of the Central Reference Library to whose staff he had become well known and liked.

Apart from this keenness for local history, he had undertaken considerable work on his own Family history and had been a member of the Birmingham & Midland Society for Genealogy & Heraldry, with which several other members of the Birmingham Medal Society were also associated. The work of this society closely relates to medal research and was of great value to him.

Because of the very considerable volume of research work undertaken by Michael Minton, it has been proposed that a Minton Memorial Award be created by the Birmingham Medal Society to be presented annually to one of its members in recognition of their research efforts. This will take the form of a bronze statuette of a soldier of the 6th Foot in the uniform of the Waterloo period.

Earlier in1993 Michael suffered some months of severe illness but appeared to be making a good recovery and had returned to work several weeks before his unexpected death. A memorial service was held on 31st December at the Robin Hood Crematorium in Hall Green Birmingham.

Michael Minton was well known for his integrity as well as for his sense of humour and will be greatly missed by both members and societies.

Reprinted with the permission from the Journal of the O.M.R.S.

Civil Defence Organisations

Prior to the outbreak of the war the Civil Defence Organisation was divided into twelve areas throughout the country, these being as follows:

No.	Designation.	Headquarters.
1.	Northern.	Newcastle.
2.	NorthEastern.	Leeds.
3.	North Midland.	Nottingham.
4.	Eastern.	Cambridge.
5.	London.	London.
6.	Southern.	Reading.
7.	South Western.	Bristol.
8.	Wales .	Cardiff.
9.	Midland.	Birmingham.
10.	NorthEastern.	Manchester.
11.	Scotland.	Edinburgh.
12.	South Eastern.	Tunbridge Wells.

To each area was appointed a Civil Defence Regional Commissioner.

For the Midland Area which covered an area from Shrewsbury to Coventry, including Birmingham this was the Earl of Dudley.

The duties of the A.R.P. Civil Defence covered such a wide range that it is not possible to give full and due credit to all concerned. Initially the main threat to the general public was thought to be that of a gas attack and with this in mind "cleansing stations" appeared at a number of the A.R.P. Depots, fortunately this threat never materialised.

The Fire Service remained at first in control of the City or County fire authorities, supplemented by the Auxiliary Fire Service. They in turn became organised on a regional basis and titled the National Fire Service with Birmingham and Coventry areas designated as Number 24. All equipment was altered to a uniform standard thus men and equipment were able to be moved to areas throughout the country, indeed the first award to a Birmingham fireman was the George Medal to Robert J. Knight for gallantry not in Birmingham but at the Royal Naval oil fuel depot at Llanreath Pembrokeshire l9th August to 5th September 1940. During the night of I9/20th November 1940 the fire service had 650 pumps engaged, whilst on the night of 22/23rd November 1940 it had 850 pumps engaged in Birmingham. The fire service was also assisted by the various work Fire Brigades.

There were also Firewatchers or Fire Guards. a number of whom died (throughout the country) when premises upon whose roofs they were stationed caught fire and means of escape destroyed. On a small local scale, street or area fire parties dealt primarily with incendiary bombs. It is of interest to note that fire service in Birmingham also formed its own Home Guard Battalion.

The Birmingham City police along with the Special Constables were later supplemented by the War Reserve Constables, and the roll of the police became very involved. Apart from normal police duties they were expected to set up "incident posts" to co-ordinate rescue work, diverting traffic around areas that had been bombed, checking reporting of unexploded bombs, protecting stocks from damaged business premises etc. A number of men received awards for service over a period of time during air raids and rescue work whilst others received a Chief Constable's Commendation, their names being Published in Police Orders for good work such as dealing with the large number of incendiaries which dropped on the city. Police Sergeant Charles Ward received the British Empire Medal for defusing a 550 pound bomb which fell into the works of Messrs Webley & Scott, Weaman Street near Steelhouse Lane on the night of 9/10th April 1941.

The Local Defence Volunteers (L.D.V) which later became the Home Guard., was formed on a County Zone basis under the style of The Royal Warwickshire Regiment. The Birmingham Battalion numbers by adding twenty became the county number, thus the 5th Birmingham Battalion became the 25th Warwickshire (Birmingham) Battalion, Home Guard. The larger businesses or organisations were able to form their own battalion whilst smaller units formed Companies or Sections and combined or amalgamated to form Battalions. Apart from guarding factories the Home Guard also manned some anti aircraft batteries. Mobile units also operated and later volunteers received instruction in bomb disposal work. The 6th Birmingham Battalion can claim to be one of the most, if not the most decorated battalion in the country, most decorations being awarded for gallantry during the bombing of the BSA works.

Many other organisations also performed outstanding work during the blitz, these include the British Red Cross, St John Ambulance Association, Womens Voluntary Services, Gas, Water and Electric Departments, R.S.P.C.A. and P.D.S.A. as did those who manned the hospitals, telephones etc.

Birmingham Civil Defence Roll of Honour

It can now be stated that 200 members of the Birmingham Civil Defence Services were killed in the City's Blitzes, and about 1,000 were injured.

Fifty received awards for conspicuous bravery:
1. George Cross.
14. George Medals.
35 British Empire Medals
44 were Commended.

B'ham Gazette, 14.11.1994, page 3.

Birmingham Auxiliary Fire Service. Roll of Honour

Date Killed.

J.H.Eaton.	B 12868.	133 Third Avenue, Small Heath.	17.10.1940.
L.Jones.	B 886.	104 Willes Road, Winson Green.	24.10.1940.
E.F.Quinn.	B 10539.	14 Dare Road, Erdington.	24.10.1940.
C.A.Perry.	B 12545.	125 St. Clements Rd., Nechells.	25.10.1940.
E.W.Payne.	B 6827.	9/23 Malt House Lane, Washwood Heath.	25.10.1940.
U.S.Kendrick.	B 13176	255 Aston Church Rd., Washwood Heath.	25.10.1940.
V.L.Clews(Hinton)	B 3453.	6/61,Wenman Street, Balsall Heath.	26.10.1940.
A.H.Lowe	B 4004	213 Rocky Lane, Perry Barr.	14.11.1940.
P.Pyett.	B 5178	24 Coniston Road, Erdington.	14.11.1940.
H.V.Lugg.	B 12760.	565 Kingstanding Rd., Erdington.	19.11.1940.
A.Cope.	B 11238.	49 St.Stephens Road, Selly Oak	19.11.1940.
.Carless.	B 12454.	51 Darley Avenue, Castle Bromwich.	20.11.1940.
R.Burrows.	B 5041.	205 Heathfield Road.	20.11.1940.
P.F.Allen.	B 6351.	24 Lincoln Street, Balsall Heath.	22/23.11.1940.
I.M.Jones.	B 13395.	21 Minyffordd, Ystalyford, Swansea	22.11.1940.
A.J.Davies.	B 11601.	275 Cateswell Road, Hall Green.	2.11.1940.
E. E. Smith	B 2894.	7 Langley Road, Small Heath.	22.11.1940.
J.E.Hibbe.rd.	B 12765.	31 Anderson Road, Erdington.	26.11.1940.
J.Markland.	B 12396.	234 Pretoria Road, South Yardley	3.12.1940.
H.Would.	B 3160.	35 Hardwick Road,, South Yardley.	3.12.1940.
D.J.Evans.	B 805	30 Brynarden Road, South Yardley	3.12.1940.
A.G.Holmes.	B 460.	23 Greswolde Road, Sparkhill	11.12.1940.
A.Shotton.	B 5155	14 Erasmus Road, Sparkbrook.	11.12.1940.
A.E.Clarke.	B 1180.	110 Esme Road, Sparkhill	11.12.1940.
L.W.Long.	B 5164.	91 Alcester Street.	11.12.1940.
F.V.Ranger.	B 2220.	19 Petersfield Road, Hall Green.	18.12.1940.
F.J.Gaskell.	B 12006	165 College Road, Moseley.	23.12.1940.
T.E.Eall.	B 12723	91 Ravenshill Road, Yardley Wood.	23.12.1940.
W.L.Tipton.	B 11401	30 Kingsthorpe Road, Kings Heath,	23.12.1940.
F.A.Hammond.	B 10364.	249 St Margarets Rd., Ward End.	8.4.1941.
G.Turner.	B 7108.	7 Brunsick Gardens, Herbert Rd, Handsworth	8.4.1941.

| S.Villers. | B 2577 | 429 Victoria Road, Aston. | 9.4.1941. |
| D.O. White. | B 2270. | 73 Barn Lane, Kings Heath. | 9.4.1941. |

Extracted from "Squirt" The journal of the Birmingham Auxiliary Fire Service. B'ham Ref Library.

Notes.

Lugg of Station 4/4 was killed by a H.E.Bomb whilst attending a fire at Holborn Hill. Hibbard of Station 4/1 was killed in a motor collision whilst in charge of a water carrying unit.

Notes:

Equipped with a silver Identification disc they were able to roam at will in the blackout (1940).

Station 5/4 was Grantham Road.

15th Birmingham (A.F.S.) Battalion Home Guard. C/O H.A.Sale M.C.,

Feb 1941 M.B.E. to Chief Officer   F. Winteringham
                                   A. L. Westcombe.

Squirt Vol 1 Feb 1940 to June 1942 L 45.611

Nov 1940	page 2&3	H. W. Coleman.	Photo/Write up.
Jan 1941	2& 3	A. Westbroock.	,,
Feb 1941	2& 3	F. Winteringham	,,
April 1941	34	Shutt (Station 6/2)	Photo
May l941	24& 25	AFS H.G.	Photo of officers.
Sept 1941	26/27/28	Green & Heath also Gammon	photo/write up
Nov 1941	12 & 13	Shutt GM	write up
Nov 1941	27	Clancy GM	write up.
Feb 1942	30.	Hasted	Photo

9th Bomb Disposal Company.
Royal Engineers.

Some idea of the work done by this unit may be gained from the fact that more than 37 Officers and men lost their lives as a result of enemy action or while removing bombs, 7 Officers and 10 Other Ranks gained awards, four Other Ranks being Commended.

It is estimated that the Company dealt with more than 1,600 large calibre bombs. The largest number of outstanding incidents at any one time waiting to be dealt with being 305 on the 24th November 1940 Their work was carried out under especially difficult conditions, apart from frequent bombings, accommodation being a particularly knotty problem to solve. When the Drill Hall in Court Oak Road, Harborne was requisitioned only a small portion could be allotted to the Company and Officers and men had to take their meals together. Yet despite frequent casualties, periods of almost continuous raids and other troubles, the members of the Company always maintained a cheerful attitude.

As far as Birmingham was concerned, there was no unit available to undertake the hazardous work of bomb disposal prior to July 1940, when the formation of the Company was commenced with a nucleus of officers and men mostly taken from Royal Engineer General Construction Companies. The first arrivals were Lieutenants Rayner and Leach and 47 Other Ranks from 726 G.C.Coy. R.E. and they were joined three weeks later, following an air raid on the City lasting five hours by a further officer, Lieutenant Campbell and another 45 Other Ranks. As time went on, more personnel arrived but, it was not until September 1st 1940 that Captain A.J.Biggs of Neath, arrived from 244 Field Coy, R.E., where he had been 2nd I/c and immediately got down to the task of forming the Company proper, with the assistance of Lieutenant C.R.Bocook, R.E. as Administration Officer. The total personnel at this time was 7 Officers and 160 Other Ranks, few enough to deal with an area including the counties of Warwickshire, Worcestershire, Herefordshire Staffordshire and Shropshire.

It was Captain Biggs who arranged certain big bangs including the explosion coming from the bottom of a hole 50 feet deep in a quarry near Oldbury. Some delayed action bombs had been unearthed by Lieutenant Rayner and his men in a residential suburb, and removed, at first, to a convenient sandpit. Even in the sandpit the bursting of the bombs might damage property, so it was decided they must be taken to the Oldbury quarry, where they could do no harm. Lieut W.E.K. Kenway, accompanied by his batman took three of the bombs, a 550 pound and two 110 pound bombs in a lorry, which he drove himself, along a circuitous route, so as to minimise the risk of damage to houses if the whole load blew up.

There, remained one other 110 pound bomb which was in a somewhat uncertain condition. With this bomb Captain Biggs himself set out on the journey to Oldbury He thought that if it rode in a lorry the bomb might be detonated by the rattling and vibration, so he had it placed in the back seat of his own private car. He took it by a selected route to the quarry, dumped it in the fifty foot hole and two or three hours later heard it detonate itself and the others already deposited there.

The Company sustained their first casualties on 31st August, 1940 when three bombs exploded during removal, killing seven Other Ranks and injuring five, one of whom died in hospital. 14th November, 1940 brought the very concentrated enemy raid on Coventry. Roads were blocked, large fires started, communications dislocated, light and gas put out of action and the raid did not cease until 6.15 am on the 15th. This was, if not the worst, one of the worst raids on any city in England. So bad was the raid that detachments were drawn from Manchester and Cardiff Companies to help in the disposal work. During this period too, it must be borne in mind that raids were still taking place in Birmingham. As early as 2nd September,1940 a raid left a legacy of 109 incidents to be dealt with, yet by the 20th only 14 unexploded bombs were outstanding. From 13th October to the 15th, raids were made daily on Coventry and Birmingham with others daily during November. It was during this month that Major General D.B.C.Taylor, Inspector of Fortifications and Director of Bomb Disposal, visited the Company and expressed great satisfaction with the methods and progress of the work which had been done, and personally congratulated Major, as he had become, A.J.Biggs. By the end of 12 months of particularly heavy bombing, the Company had dealt with 2,174 incidents and there only being 23 unexploded bombs, all in category 'D' outstanding.

This good work was recognised when the following awards to members of the Company were notified in the London Gazette; George Cross; Lieut. A.F.N.Campbell and Sergeant M.C.Gibson; George Medal; Major A,J.Biggs, Lieut L.C.Meynell, D.S.F. Rayner and R.H.Lee and Lance Sergeant J.H.Hinton. British Empire Medals to Sergeant E.C.Oxford and Sapper H.W.Carman. King's Commendations to Sappers J.Todd and J.E.Brown. Lieut D.H.Anderson was made a Member of the British Empire and Sergeant K.Ashton was also awarded the British Empire Medal in the Birthday Honours list in July 1941.

At the same time a special badge was granted to Bomb Disposal Units, to be worn on the left sleeve.

By the 29th February 1941 the Company had dealt with 2,290 incidents. Then there came a welcome lull broken on the 8th April 1941 by a further concentrated raid on Coventry. The following day, a concentrated raid was made on Birmingham. Both cities had yet another raid on the 10th.By the 13th April there was quite a lot of work on hand and six Auxiliary Bomb Disposal Squads, Home Guard from Austin Motors Ltd. commenced bomb disposal work under the supervision of the Company Commander. Four firms in Birmingham sent members of their Auxiliary Bomb Disposal Squads for practice training. Enemy activity continued at intervals during the next few months and the work of the Company had more gratifying recognition in the following awards, which were announced at the end of September.

George Medals to Captain T.H.Sharman, Sergeant E.Laing and A.Sanders. Corporal W.Hone,and Lance Corporal E.W.Suttle. British Empire Medals; Lance Sergeant H. Elliott and Corporal A.E.Green. King's Commendations went to two men whose names are not learned.

In order to commemorate the Officers and Men of the unit who lost their lives while employed on Bomb Disposal duties in 1940 and 1941, two large oak candlesticks were purchased by the Company and installed in St. Faith's Church, (later the Parish Church of St.Faith and St.Laurence), Harborne where the Company had held a parade service weekly during the past three years. Many Officers who had served with the unit during the "Blitz's" returned for the Dedication Ceremony, chief of them being Major A.J.Biggs.G.M., who had commanded the Company in 1940-1941.The Rev W.Sissons conducted the service, and a short but impressive dedication ceremony was carried out by Major, The Rev Alex Birkmire, Senior Chaplain to the Forces, Birmingham Area. At the end of the service, which was held on the 7th November 1943 officers and men of the Company filed slowly past in remembrance of their lost comrades.

"We want your bombs" is their heroic motto

The following article appeared in "The Birmingham Gazette 18th September 1940.

We want your bombs, that death defying motto, chalked by hand of some unknown hero on the sides of a military lorry seen yesterday in a Midland town, typifies the spirit of the men of the Bomb Disposal Sections of the Royal Engineers who have just won the world wide admiration by their removal of the huge bomb which threatened St. Pauls Cathedral with destruction.

Because it was one of the worlds great cathedrals which was endangered their heroism has, of course attracted single attention, but deeds of equal devotion and bravery performed in less spectacular circumstances by other officers and men of the sections must not be overlooked.

Early in the raiding season the Midland Region had three of these sections under the command of Lieut. D.S.F. Rayner, formerly a Territorial, whose home is in Birmingham.

It was a party of his men, in charge of Sergeant Bodsworth, of Thorpe Street Drill Hall, Birmingham, who investigated a small hole in a field near Redditch. The hole was believed to contain a delayed action bomb and as it had been there for three days it could be expected to blow up at any moment.

The Sappers nevertheless, dug down in search of the bomb, found it at last about

20 feet below the ground and heard it's clock work fuse still ticking.

It was a 500 pound bomb so any one may guess what would have happened to Sgt Bodsworth and his party if, the bomb had done it's worst at that moment, or if they had accidentally touched it off.

They removed the fuse and carted the bomb away for examination by other interested experts.

Subsequently a large number of unexploded bombs were reported from various districts of the Midland Region. Some of them were creatures of the imagination, but others were far from being harmless. All of them had to be investigated and Capt. A. J. Biggs R.E. of Neath came with reinforcements for the disposal parties.

Captain Biggs "arranged" the innocuousness of certain big bangs that were heard one evening by most people in the Birmingham area. The explosions came from the bottom of a hole 50 foot deep in a quarry near Oldbury.

Some delayed action bombs had been unearthed by Lieut Rayner and his men in a residential suburb and removed at first, to a convenient sandpit, lest their explosion wreck houses near the spot where they had fallen.

The R.E.s then thought that even in the sandpit the bursting of the bombs might damage property, so it was decided they must be taken away to the Oldbury quarry, where they could do no harm at all.

Lieut Kenway, accompanied by his batman. Took three of the bombs a 500 pound and two of 110 pound in a lorry, which he drove himself along a circuitous route, so as to minimise the risk of damage to houses if the whole load blew up.

There remained one other 110 pound bomb which, owing to a mischance during it's previous treatment, was in a somewhat uncertain condition.

With this bomb Capt. Biggs himself set out on the seven mile journey to Oldbury.

He rather thought that if it rode in a lorry the bomb might be detonated by the rattling and vibration to which lorries are prone, so he had it placed in the back seat of his own private car. He took it by a selected route to the quarry, dumped it in the fifty foot hole, and two or three hours later heard it detonate itself and the others already deposited there.

The Disposal Company has not done its work without grievous loss. A party of Sappers had dug down to a bomb and were looking it over, when they heard a fizzing sound. They retreated for a few minutes, but a water works employee then told them that the fizzing had come from a punctured water main.

They accordingly returned to the crater they had dug and two of the men went down to tackle the bomb once again, while others watched them from above. At this very moment the bomb exploded.

Seven men were killed on the spot, another was fatally injured.
These were: -

Corporal R.Haines
Driver M.T.Andrews
Sappers N. Cryer
W.W.Davies
R.Haines
W.E.Fergusson
A.Knight.
W.E.Thorn

Lance Corporal W.Dawson. Driver J.E.Ablet and Sappers J.C.Cottrell and W.Hardy are still in hospital.

Shoulder Flash and Unit Badge of Warwickshire Home Guard.

HONOURS AND AWARDS
9th BOMB DISPOSAL COMPANY ROYAL ENGINEERS.

GEORGE CROSS

2nd Lieut. Alexander Fraser Campbell

4445289   Sgt. Michael Gibson.

GEORGE MEDAL

	Capt. Alfred John Biggs	22 01 41
2021663	L/Sgt John Henry Hinton	22 01 41
1880443	Cpl William Hone	30 09 41
2217011	Sgt Edward Laing	30 09 41
	2nd Lieut. Ralph Henry Lee Bsc.	22 01 41
	Lieut Lionel Charles Maynell	17 12 40
	Lieut Douglas Stanley Frederick Rayner	22 01 41
2074517	L/Sgt Andrew Sanders	30 09 41
	Capt. Thomas Henry Sharman	30 09 41
1883145	L/Cpl Ernest William Suttle.	30 09 41

M.B.E.

2nd Lieut. Derek Hawdey Anderson.   21 01 41

B.E.M.

1914139	Sgt Kenneth Ashton	01 07 41
2036910	L/GGt Horace Elliott	30 09 41
2014169	Driver Arthur Ellis Green	30 09 41
1920394	Cpl. Edward Charles Oxford	22 01 41
2090614	Sapper Henry William Carman	

KING'S COMMENDATION

2196474	Sapper John Edward Brown
1942454	Sapper John Todd.

Mine Disposal

The mines dropped during the air raids were designed for parachuting into the shipping lanes of the Channel and major seaports. When first used the responsibility for dealing with them fell to The Directorate of Torpedoes and Mining, of the Admiralty. Due to the shortage of heavy calibre bombs, the Germans used them as blast bombs on land. The Royal Navy however, were still responsible for defusing and removal of those which failed to explode.

Men from this dedicated Naval unit came not only from the Royal Navy and Royal Naval Volunteer Reserve, but also from the Royal Australian Naval Volunteer Reserve, as well as others. However, the full exploits of these men and their work during the Birmingham Blitz may never be fully learned, for many of these men not only carried on their vital work in Birmingham and Coventry, but also as far away as Glasgow, Cardiff, Liverpool and the London area etc,

Parachute mines fell in the centre of the City, some near Steelhouse Lane and immediate area, but many fell in the residential suburban areas devastating much property in densely, packed areas. During the air raid of Wednesday 11th and Thursday 12th December1940 five parachute mines fell in the Handsworth area and exploded in Albert Road, Douglas Road and Charles Street also a number of high explosive bombs and incendiaries. In addition to the mines, which exploded on impact, two unexploded mines fell. One at the rear of 28 Queens Head Road and the other in the allotments at the junction of Friary Road and Oxhill Road, according to police reports. In the case of the mine which fell in Queens Head Road this exploded in the afternoon of the 12th December when being removed by the Naval Authorities but the number of casualties was not disclosed. The other was successfully removed without incident on the 14th. In both cases a large number of people, over a wide area had to be evacuated.

It was Temporary Electrical Lieut. Stanley Edmund Jenner of the Royal Australian Naval Reserve who dealt not only with the mine, which fell near the Royal Air Force Station at Wythall, just over the city boundary, in November 1940 but also two others which fell in Coventry. For which he was in June, 1941 awarded the George Medal. In the Coventry area, he was assisted by A.B.Tucker G.C. In mid December 1940 Lieut. Howard D.Reid in Birmingham was rendering a mine safe and whilst dealing with it the fuse started but he returned to it and finished the operation successfully.

For this and another which fell in Cardiff, the latter being also dealt with by Tucker G.C. and Seaman John McFetridge, Royal Naval Reserve, being of a very difficult nature was awarded the George Medal in 1941.

It was Lieut. William H.Taylor G.C., who came to Birmingham in late 1940, who was asked to tackle a mine lying on the surface at the junction of Burberry

Street and Gerrard Street. Whilst inspecting the mine from a safe distance he became aware that one of his colleagues Lieut John R.Rouson had already commenced work on it. He had started the fuse ticking and had run for cover, when Taylor turned up, together they tried again but they bent the spanners and dislocated Rouson's thumb. At last they came to the conclusion that they had no choice but to abandon the mine, as it could not be moved due to its dangerous condition and to explode it. They thought it best to set fire to it, a considerable portion of the charge should be burnt before the fire reached the detonators, providing the fuse did not operate before then. After an enormous flare up the mine exploded leaving them both bruised and shaken. Later, at Reginald Street, Saltley an unexploded mine was found standing vertically and partly buried about three steps up the staircase of a tenement building. Again both men worked together, it was not possible to start the locking ring and the fuse started ticking, they ran for their lives, the mine exploded and damaged thirty to forty houses. Both men were wounded and taken to hospital. Ordinary Seaman Wilson Boyce R.N. was associated and worked with both Rouson and Taylor. Rouson and Boyce both received the George Medal, whilst Taylor had already been awarded the George Cross for his work at Uxbridge R.A.F. Depot.

Lieut James H. Kessack of the Royal Australian Naval Volunteer Reserve dealt with his first mine, one that had fallen into a Birmingham clubroom on the 14th December 1940. With the assistance of John McFetridge, Royal Naval Reserve, and Thomas Novis, Royal Navy, they gained access to the fuse and successfully rendered it safe. For this and dealing with mines elsewhere all three received the George Medal. Kessack regretfully lost his life while attempting to render a mine safe on 28th April 1941 in Glasgow. Novis was awarded his medal for mine disposal at St.James' East London.

As with awards to the men of Bomb Disposal, the London Gazette invariably states citation as "For conspicuous gallantry in carrying out hazardous work in a very brave manner". It is only from the recommendations or reports that the details of award may be gleaned, and these may involve two or three incidents as well as other men.

Regretfully, the names of those who received other awards or commendations, let alone those who served or were casualties have not been learned.

For details of Handsworth mines see recommendation of Police Inspector Harold Whittall.

The George Cross

The original warrant of September 1940 instituting the George Cross was cancelled by a new warrant in May 1941. The decoration consists of a plain silver cross with a circular medallion in the centre bearing a representation of St.George and the Dragon surrounded by the words FOR GALLANTRY .In the angle of each limb of the cross is the Royal cypher GVI. The reverse is plain and bears the name of the recipient and date of award. The cross is suspended by a ring from a silver bar, adorned with laurel leaves. The ribbon is dark blue.

The George Cross, which may be awarded posthumously is intended primarily for civilians and award to members of the fighting services is confined to actions for which purely military honours are not normally granted. Recipients are entitled to the use of the letters G.C. after their name.

The George Medal

This medal was instituted in 1940 and the obverse bears the effigy of the Sovereign. The reverse depicts St. George slaying the Dragon on the coast of England, circumscribed by the words THE GEORGE MEDAL. The medal is named on the rim and is suspended by a red ribbon with five equal narrow vertical blue stripes. Recipients are entitled to use the letters G.M after their name.

The Defence Medal

This medal was granted for three years service, between 3rd September 1939 and 8th May 1945 in Great Britain. In the case of mine and bomb disposal in the forces, the time qualification was three months.

Amongst the categories eligible;

Members of the forces who had served in the United Kingdom, personnel of Anti Aircraft Commands, the Home Guard, Wardens Service and Shelter Wardens, Rescue Service, Messenger Service, Ambulance Service, First Aid Services, First Aid Posts Nursing Service, Rest Centre Service, Canteen Service, Mortuary Service, National Fire Service (including local authority Fire Brigade and Auxiliary -fire Service), Police. Civil Nursing Reserve. Nurses in hospitals for which Government or local authorities are responsible, Fire Guards, performing duties under the local authorities or at Government premises etc.

The medal is cupro, nickel, with on the obverse the uncrowned Head of King George V1, the reverse, a coat of arms with the dates1939 and 1945 to either side, beneath the words The Defence Medal.

The medal was issued un-named.

The Edward Medal

This medal was established in 1907 for distinguishing heroic acts performed by miners and quarrymen who endanger their own lives in saving or endeavouring to save the lives of others. In 1909 this was extended to those who, in the course of industrial employment endangered their lives in saving or endeavouring to save the lives of others from danger incurred in connection with such industrial employment. The medals are of silver and bronze and the obverse of both bear the Royal effigy, the reverse of the miners and quarrymen's medal shows a miner rescuing a comrade and has the words FOR COURAGE. The reverse of the industrial medal shows a classical female figure holding a wreath and the words FOR COURAGE and the outline of a town or city in the background. The medal is suspended by a dark blue ribbon with narrow yellow borders and is named on the rim.

These medals were later exchanged for the George Cross.

The Most Excellent Order of the British Empire

This was founded by King George V in 1917 for services to the Empire at home and in the Dominions and Colonies. It could be conferred upon officers of the fighting services of a non-combatant character. The Military Division can be conferred upon members of the fighting services which do not qualify them for other order or decoration for services in the field or before the enemy. During the 1939-1943 War the Order was frequently conferred for service in action.

The star of the Order (O.B.E.) is silver gilt. In the centre, within a circle are the conjoint busts of King George V and Queen Mary facing left. The circle contains the motto "For God and The Empire." The Members Star (M.B.E) is silver and is identical to the Order.

The Medal of the Order of the British Empire for Meritorious Service is silver. The obverse has a representation of Britannia with the motto of the Order ,and in the exergue the words For Meritorious Service. The reverse has the Royal and Imperial cypher of the Sovereign and the words Instituted by King George. The medal suspender is ornamented with oak leaves, it is named on the rim. This medal is awarded both for gallantry and meritorious service.

The ribbon is rose pink edged with pearl grey for the Civil awards, a narrow central stripe being added for the ribbon of the Military awards.

The King's Commendation for Brave Conduct

The award corresponds roughly to a "civilian" mention in despatches for gallantry. The emblem is worn on the appropriate medal or if no medal has been awarded on the coat after any other medals or ribbons. If none has been awarded the emblem is worn in the position where a medal or single ribbon would be worn. Certificates accompany the award of a commendation. The emblem from about 1943 was a plastic badge, gold coloured. Being an upright sword with a crown at the top, a wreath from the sword hilt to the crown the voided portion with the wreath being red. In the centre are the words For Brave Conduct. Later, this emblem was replaced by a silver oak leaf.

Apart from the above, the No.9 Regional Commissioner, the Earl of Dudley sent letters of commendation, whilst the police would be mentioned or commended in Police Orders, issued by the Chief Constable. Many of the latter appear to be for extinguishing incendiary bombs or good work during an air raid.

The King's Police Medal

This medal was instituted in 1909 for award to officers of police and fire brigades throughout the Dominions for conspicuous gallantry, distinguished administration or organising work, special or valuable services etc. This silver medal has the Sovereign's effigy and legend on the obverse, on the reverse a watchman leaning on a sword and holding a shield inscribed "To Guard My People", with the outline of a city or town in the background. The ribbon is dark blue with white edges with a white stripe in the centre. Since 1933 there has been two distinct medals "For Gallantry" and "For Distinguished Service". The first has the words "For Gallantry" in the exergue at the foot of the figure, while a thin red line was added to each white stripe. The second retains the old ribbon but the medal has the words "For Distinguished service". The medal became known as the King's Police and Fire Service Medal during the war 1939 to 1945.This became the Queen's Police Medal in May 1954,and a separate medal was instituted for the Fire Services. The Queen's Police Medal for Gallantry is now only awarded posthumously.

The Life Saving Medal of The Order of St John

By Dr L.Lloyd
This medal instituted in 1874, is awarded in silver and bronze and there are two types. The first type issued during the period 1874-1888 has on its obverse the Badge of the Order without embellishment, surrounded by the words AWARDED BY THE ORDER OF ST JOHN OF JERUSALEM IN ENGLAND and the reverse, a sprig of St John's Wort with scrolls bearing the words "JERUSALEM, ACRE, CYPRUS, RHODES, and MALTA". This is surrounded by the words FOR SERVICE IN THE CAUSE OF HUMANITY.

The second type, from 1888 has on the obverse, the Badge of the Order, embellished, surrounded by the words FOR SERVICE IN THE CAUSE OF

HUMANITY. The reverse a sprig of St John's Wort with the scrolls bearing the words JERUSALEM and ENGLAND surrounded by the words AWARDED BY THE GRAND PRIORY OF THE HOSPITAL OF ST.JOHN OF JERUSALEM IN ENGLAND. The medal is suspended by a black ribbon.

1892   The issues of bars to the medal for additional acts of gallantry was approved and when so awarded are in the same metal as the medal itself.

Bars to the medal
        Rectangular in shape 1.5 inches by 0.25 inches with the badge of the Order in a circle in the centre (embellished) with oak leaves on each side.

1907   Gold Medals were authorised

The Ribbon
1874-1888
        A black unwatered ribbon, 1.25 inches (3.2 cms) wide with the badge of the Order not embellished, woven within the ribbon or embroidered on the ribbon in white.

1888-1950
        A black watered ribbon 1.25 inches for early awards increasing to 1.5 inches for later awards.

1950-1954
        A black watered ribbon 1.5 inches (3.8 cms) wide with scarlet (outer) and white (inner) stripes at each side.

1954- to date
        A black watered ribbon 1.6 inches (4.1 cms) wide with scarlet (outer) and white (inner) stripes at each side but separated by a narrow black line.

Badge for the King's "Commended"

The King has approved a badge for issue to those granted civil Commendations for brave conduct.

It has been designed by Mr. Kruger Gray, part designer of the George Cross and Medal and will be sent during the next few Weeks to all those to whom Civil Commendations have already been awarded.

The Badge is intended to be worn in plain clothes on the left lapel on the coat, or in a corresponding position.

In the Merchant Navy, Civil Defence, Police, National Fire Service and other Civilian Uniforms it should be placed immediately above the centre of the position in which any medal ribbons are worn.

The Badge will be sent to the next of kin of those granted posthumous civil commendations for brave conduct, but not for wear.

Description
From about 1943 a plastic badge was issued to denote a civil commendation. The badge is gold coloured, the voided portion within the wreath being red. Later this was replaced by a silver oak leaf which is similar to the miniature version worn on the ribbon of the Empire Gallantry Medal (q.v.) between 1933 and 1940. The first issues were made with two prongs at the back for fixing to the ribbon or to the coat, but are now made with a brooch fitting.

Special Constabulary Long Service Medal

Established by King George V in 1918 in consideration of the faithful and devoted service of the Special Constabulary during the First World War and also of providing a means of recognising continued and efficient service in the future. During the two world wars, to qualify a special constable must have served without pay for not less than three years and during that period have performed at least fifty police duties a year and be recommended by a chief officer as willing and competent to discharge duties as required. In Peace the medal is granted after nine years service provided the fifty duties a year have been performed, and the person recommended. Service in both world wars counts treble.

The medal is bronze having on the obverse the Sovereign's effigy, obverse has the inscription For Faithful Service in The Special Constabulary, half surrounded from bottom to right by a semi-circular spray of laurel. A bar, The Great War 1914-18 was awarded to the medal to these who qualified. Bars worded Long Service are awarded for each successive period of ten years provided the fifty duties a year have been performed. The medal is named on the rim.

The Royal Society for the Prevention of Cruelty to Animals.

From the proposal to recognise distinguished service came in 1907, the award of silver and bronze medals for animal life saving, followed later by the institution of the Margaret Wheatley Cross, named after Miss Margaret Wheatley, aged 16 years who gave her life for a dog in June, 1936.

Margaret Wheatley Cross; this is the highest award by the Society and consists of a small bronze cross with its name and date of institution on the obverse. It is suspended by a dark blue ribbon with a white stripe near the edges, and with a top bronze bar.

Silver and Bronze medals; these medals are identical except one being of silver and the other bronze. A female seated figure with animals either side and underneath the words R.S.P.C.A. On the obverse. On the reverse, in the centre, a coat of arms, with the words around the outside Royal Society for the Prevention of Cruelty to Animals. Underneath the coat of arms the words For Animal Life Saving. The ribbon of the silver medal is blue with white stripes whilst that of the bronze medal also has two red stripes.

The cross is named on the obverse and the silver and bronze medals are named and dated on the rim.

Mike Minton archives volumes 32. 33. 34.

PLACES and DATES OF INCIDENTS.

PLACE.		DATE
2	Telephone house	27th August 1940
3	River Rea	27th August 1940
4	R.S.P.C.A. Hospital. Bristol Street	1940
5	310, Birchfield Road Perry Barr	
6	Temp. Telephone Exchange Castle Bromwich	
7	Bordesley Railway Junction	26/27th August 1940
8	Air Raids, Erdington, Castle Bromwich	
	Tyburn Road, Aston Road North	9th Aug 1940 - January 1941
9	Aeroplane Factory Castle Bromwich	3rd September 1940
10	Location unknown	6th September 1940
11	Ryvita Factory Bordesley Green	9th September 1940
	G.E.C. works Witton	20th November 1940
	B.S.A. Guns Ltd	28th November 1940
12	Curzon Street L.M.S. Railway	15th October 1940
13	Bishop Street Edgbaston	15/16th October 1940
14	First Aid Post. Kent Street Baths	26th October 1940
15	Brearley Street/Summer Lane	26th October 1940
16	Moseley Area (Heathfield hotel)	October 1940
17	Anti Aircraft Gun Site	Unknown
18	Rowton House. Alcester Street	15/16th October 1940
	Birchall street	4th December 1940
	Ravenhurst Street	4th December 1940

	Vaughan Street Highgate	10th April 1941
	Artillery Street Bordesley	17th May 1941
19	Knowle Road Sparkhill	17th October 1940
20	Stechford Area	17th October 1940
21	Edgbaston Area	18th October 1940
22	G.E.C Works. Electric Avenue Witton.	19th October 1940
	B.S.A.Guns Ltd	12th November 1940
	Wolseley Motors Factory. Drews Lane, Washford Heath.	10th April 1941
36	Grant Street. Lee Bank	19th October 1940
37	St. Paul's Road, BaIsall Heath	19th November 1940
38	Ashley Street off Bristol Street	19th November 1940
39	Tenby Street North	ditto
40	Queen's Hospital. Bath Row	ditto
41	St. George's Street (between Hampton Street	
	and Hospital Street) Hockley	ditto
42	B.S.A. Guns Ltd. Small Heath	19/20th November 1940
43	Hope Street Birmingham 5	ditto
44	98, Murdock Road. Handsworth	ditto
45	Nechells Gas Works	
	Dolobran Road Sparkbrook	ditto
46	Burbury Street/Gerrard Street Saltley	ditto
	Reginald Street	
47	Post Office Depot	22/23rd November 1940
48	Premises of William Mc Geoch & Co. Ltd.	ditto
	Coventry Road Camp Hill	ditto
49	Gas Holder Washwood Heath, Saltley	22/23rd November 1940
50	110 Yardley Wood Road	23rd November 1940
	Granthan Road A.F.Station. Sparkbrook	11th December 1940
51	Coventry Road-Whitmore Road Stables	23rd November 1940
52	Daimler Factory Coventry	14th November 1940
	Highgate Common. Birmingham	24th November 1940
53	Singer Motor Works	27th November 1940
	B.S.A. Guns Ltd Small Heath	12th December 1940
54	Great Russell Street. Hockley	4th December 1940
55	A.R.P. Depot Kings Road Tyseley	11th December 1940
56	Digbeth	
57	Windsor Road. Lifford, Kings Norton	12th December 1940
58	Clubroom, Birmingham. Area unknown	
	Mine Disposal	14th December 1940
59	Location Unknown mine Disposal	Mid December 1940

60	Olton Boulevard, Acock's Green. Mine disposal	16th December 1940
61	Yardley, Stechford, Aston	August. October
	Nechells Power Station. Witton Area	December 1940
62	Ladywood/ Edgbaston Street	October 1940 to Feb 41
63	Handsworth Area.	Oct. Nov. Dec. 1940
64	Location not known	1940
65	Washwood Heath Road.St Margarets road near	
	Bromford Lane	9th April 1941
66	Summer Lane	9th April 1941
67	Garrison Lane (Block of flats)	9/10th April 1941
68	Washwood Heath sidings	9/10th April 1941
69	Ravenhurst Street. Broom Street	9/10th April 1941
70	L. H. Newton & Co Ltd. works	9/10th April 1941
71	Abbotsford Road, Sparkbrook	9/10th April 1941
72	Miller Street Tram Depot	9/10/11th April 1941
73	Unknown	
74	Osborn Road, Sparkhill	10th April 1941
75	Scotland Street, Ladywood	10th April 1941
76	Webley & Scott. Weaman Street	10th April 1941
77	Golden Hillock Road. Sparkbrook	10th April 1941
78	Lawden Street. Small Heath	10th April 1941
79	Ward End Road. Off Drews Lane	10th April 1941
80	Trevor Street. Premises of Prostans,	
	Morley Bros & Birtles Ltd. Paint Varnish	10th April 1941
	& Oil Manufacturers.	
81	Bertram Road. Small Heath	10th April 1941
82	Hockley Hill	11th April 1941
83	Bus Park Garrison Lane	10/11th April 1941
84	128–130, City Road	11th April 1941
85	Edgbaston / Basall Heath Area	Unknown
86	Tyburn Road Erdington	
87	155–164 Scholefield Nechells	17th May 1941
88	Great Hampton Street Hockley St. Area	28th July 1942
89	Gabriels Ltd. Coleshill Street	28th July 1942
90	St. Andrews junction Box. Duddeston	30th July 1942
91	Pheasey Farm Grenade Range	29th November 1942

Blitz Statistics - Birmingham

Ref. Clem Lewis. Birmingham Mail
Birmingham was the third most heavily bombed City in Britain
August 1940 - April 1941 - Birmingham suffered a series of severe air raids

High Explosive Bombs	5129
Parachute Land Mines	48
Incendiary Bombs	numerous
H.E.Bombs per 10 acres of city	1
Persons Killed	2241
Seriously injured	3010
Slightly injured	3682
Factories destroyed	99
Factories demolished	184
Houses damaged	100, 000
Houses demolished	4500
No. of air raids	63
Numerous air raid warnings	
Tonnage of bombs dropped on Birmingham	1800

Blitz Statistics - Birmingham

B'ham Gazette 26th September 1944.

Fatal Casualties in the 77 German air raids on Birmingham were 2,227 it may now be revealed for the first time. There were 3,021 people seriously injured and 3,689 slightly hurt.

The heaviest raid in casualties was that on 19th-20th November 1940 when 615 people lost their lives, with 542 seriously injured and practically the same number slightly hurt.

In the next heaviest raid, that of 9th-10th April 1941 350 people were killed and 428 seriously injured. Again the number who received minor injuries was almost the same figure.

Ten thousand houses were completely destroyed in all the raids and well over 100,000 damaged in some respect about one in three of all the houses in the City.

Some of the most extensive damage was done by land mines. Direct hits on public shelters were fortunately few and about 20 casualties was the highest number suffered from this cause.

After one raid four fifths of the City was without water. The longest raid was 13 hours.

In the raid of 9th-10th April 1941, the number of fires was proportionate to the worst London had to face on any single night.

NB: Slight difference between statistics published by The Birmingham Mail and The Birmingham Gazette could be accounted for by injured civilians later dying and by injuries coming to light at different dates.

B.S.A. Guns Ltd. Small Heath
Night of 19/20th November 1940

Honours and Awards

George Medals

Albert William Bailey	Volunteer. 6th Birmingham Battalion
L.G. 11.2.1941	
John Hadley	A.R.P. Rescue Party
L.G.11.4.1941	
Alfred Frank Stevens	Works Electrician. B.S.A.Guns Ltd.
L.G.17.1.1941	

British Empire Medal

Arthur Richard Edmund Harris	Works Pipe Fitter. B.S.A. Guns Ltd.
Alfred Walter Goodwin	Works Electrician. B.S.A. Guns Ltd.
L.G.17.1.1941	
John Hastings Beattie	Sub Section Leader.
Joseph Topham	Section Leader.
William Saragine.	Volunteer.
L.G.17.1.1941	All 6th Birmingham Battalion. Home Guard.

King's Commendation

Samuel Simpton Ashburner	Works Fitter.
Edwyn Hoof	Works Electrician.
Ernest Williams	Works Browner.
L.G.17.1.1941	All of B.S.A. Guns Ltd.
Frank Knight	
George John Treen	All Volunteers, 6th Birmingham.
George Wilson	Battalion. Home Guard.
L.G.11.2.1941	

New Years Honours. 9th January 1946
Member of the British Empire (Civil)

Miss Ada Mary Deeming	Matron B.S.A. Co.Ltd.

British Empire Medal (Civil)

Albert Slim	Grinder B.S.A. Co.Ltd.

Buried in the ruins of B.S.A. 19th November 1940

I was lying on a bench, sharing it with two other men and listening to the accordion player, when suddenly there came a dull thud. Bright lights stabbed the darkness for a second. Then followed a rumbling noise as if the whole building were crumbling. The one thing we had always feared had come about. There had been a direct hit.

What happened next, I don't know, for I must have been knocked out. When I recovered consciousness, I found myself still lying at the end of my form. My two companions however, were on the floor, crushed to death under a steel girder. Had that girder been straight I should have been killed too, but it was curved and the curve, which was a few inches above my chest, was keeping a mass of debris from falling on me. One of my feet was held fast by a piece of steelwork, and it took me an hour of desperate struggling before I managed to wrench it free. And as I struggled, there came from all parts of the basement shouts for help mingled with the groans of the injured and the dying. But once my foot was free I was no better off, that we were all doomed. I joined in the shouts for help, but little did we realize the mountains of ruins above us. No one from the outside could possibly hear our cries.

To add to our plight, fire broke out. There could be no escape now, I sat there watching the flames, wondering how long it would be before everything around me would be alight. Presently I noticed that, in falling a machine had formed a small arch. Under this I wriggled-at least I would be safe from anything that might fall. The fire was now burning the form on which I had been sitting. The shouting and the groaning were stilling into the strange hush of death.

The smoke began to get down my throat, Then I felt a trickle of water falling on me. I realised that firemen were at work with the hoses. But it was hopeless! I began to pray. Suddenly I noticed that the smoke was blowing away from me and that the air was clearing. I realised that if I kept under the arch the fire would burn away from me. This calmed me and I decided to have a smoke, I still had my pipe and after a lot of twisting I got my tobacco and my matches from my pocket. The tobacco was fairly dry although by now I was soaked through by water from above. I filled my pipe but the matches were damp. I held them near a hot cinder until they caught alight. That first puff at my pipe was wonderful. Water was now beginning to collect on the concrete floor on which I was half sitting, half lying.

Hour by hour went by. Sometimes I shouted for help but not often, it was too exhausting. The silence was almost terrifying. There was no groaning from the other victims now. Suddenly, after one bout of shouting I thought I could hear an answering cry. I became frantic and shouted still louder. I listened, I was right. Faintly I could hear someone answering me but the voice sounded miles away. Gradually they became clearer and after a while I could make out they were asking me where I was. I shouted my position, I could hear them telling me to keep my spirits up.

Then there were tumbling noises above me and I realised they were moving wreckage to get at me. I waited. It seemed like hours, Why didn't they hurry?. Little did I know the amount of debris they had to shift. I was excited and kept on calling out to them. Then I could hear them shouting down a small hole, almost over me. They asked me if I was injured or crushed. I told them I was alright except for the fire. Then they started to cut away the twisted metal and machinery until they could see the light from my torch. Within half an hour they had managed to make a hole over me through which I could have squeezed, but I had to tell them that I could not stand up and that I was pinned in. They burned away more metal and then dropped down a rope. I caught hold of it and they pulled me up until my head was through the hole. Then they grabbed my arms and dragged me through to freedom. I asked the time; it was 5-45 I had been down there for more than nine hours.*

Award of King's Commendation, for which no date or location of incident has been traced.

Miss Georgina Nelly Adams	A.R.P. Warden.
L.G.14.3.1941	
Leslie Joseph Arkinstall	Auxiliary Fireman A.F.S.
L.G. 21.2.1941	
Harold Emery.	Member Works Fire Brigade.
L.G. 7.3.1941	
James Henry Fitzgerald	Works Maintenance engineer.
L.G.17.1.1941	
William Ford	A.R.P. Section Warden.
L.G.14.3.1941	
David Gumbley	Fitters Mate.
James Gumbley	Millwright.
L.G.14.3.1941	
James Edward Hayward	Member Works Fire Brigade.
L.G.7.3.1941	
Wilfred Ketley	Tinsmith.
L.G.7.3.1941.	
William James Larcombe.	Technical Advisor.
L.G..20.12.1942	Civil Defence.
Robert Henry Llewellyn.	Member, Works Fire Brigade.
L.G.7.3.1941	
Richard Wilfred Martin	Chief Fireman Works A.F.S.
L.G.25.4.1941	
Albert Mayne	Section Officer A.F.S.
L.G.25.4.1942	

* Extract from "A History of Industry in Birmingham" © Marie B. Rowlands

Ronald Charles Phillips	Messenger. Civil Defence.
L.G.25.9.1942	Wardens Service.
Cyril John Potter	Deputy Head A.R.P. Warden.
L.G.21.3.1941	
Mrs Ada Louise Rose	A.R.P. Warden.
L.G.12.12.1940	
Harold Shepherd.	Fire Watcher A.R.P.
L.G.3.1.1941	organisation.
Howell Thomas	A.R.P. Sector Warden
L.G.7.3.1941	
Norman Whalley.	Probationary Police Constable.
L.G.25.9.1942	
Hardy Whitehouse	Commissionaire, Night A.R.P
L.G.24.1.1941	Warden.
Patrick Walter Wilkie	Demolition Foreman.
L.G 30.1.1941	
Mrs Irene Rachel Williams.	Staff Warden, Civil Defence.
L.G. 25.2.1942.	
Charles Patrick Wright	A.R.P. Motor Despatch Rider.
L.G.14.2.1941.	

If anyone has information regarding any of these people, will you please contact:
Mrs Margaret Fisher, 72 Shirley Road, Acocks Green, Birmingham B27 7NA.
Telephone 0121 706 9621. E-mail: margaret@swan51freeserve.co.uk

Raid 25th – 26th August 1940

S.M.G & Certificate R.S.P.C.A: Victor Leverington & Edgar Garfield.
B.M.G & Certificate R.S.P.C.A: Frank Bennett.
M.W.C: Marion E. Almond & Maurice Jones

The award of a Silver Medal for Gallantry in saving Animals and Certificate of the Royal Society for the Prevention Cruelty to Animals, to Victor Leverington and Edgar Garfield. The award of a Bronze medal and Certificate for Gallantry in Saving Animals Lives to Frank Bennett and the award of a Margaret Wheatley Cross to Miss Marion E. Almond and Mr Maurice Jones

From the Birmingham Gazette, 3rd March 1941
R.S.P.C.A HOSPITAL
No George Cross citation makes more graphic reading than the story of heroism told in Birmingham yesterday, when two R.S.P.C.A officials, Miss Marion E. Almond and Mr Maurice Jones, received the Society's highest award, the Margaret Wheatley Cross and Certificate for rescue work during one of the city's heaviest raids.

On duty at an R.S.P.C.A hospital, they had over many hours, extinguished some 60 incendiaries with the aid of Mr Jones' brother, and rendered first aid to firemen and other people when, it was stated, the position became "nearly desperate".
With premises burning fiercely all around, they decided that the 26 creatures inside

Leverington, Garfield, Almond and Bennet[1]

---
[1] Pic - Presentation to recipients, Birmingham Gazette 3rd March 1941

– all evacuees from bombed homes – could stay no longer.

So 17 cats eight dogs and a canary, all in a terrified condition. were loaded into an ambulance and taken out of the town to other kennels and pens.

So difficult was the four-mile journey that it occupied two hours and at many points they were allowed by the police to proceed only at their own risk.

The Lord Mayor (Alderman Martineau) handed over the awards in the Lord Mayor's parlour.

MARKET HALL RESCUES

Police-constable Richard Tunstall received a silver medal and certificate for rescuing a dog trapped in a manhole. He was off duty when he descended the manhole in Hunter's Vale – one of the deepest portions of the Hockley Brook area – and walked along the brook under Villa Street and Wellesley Street. He took the dog home and fed it then handed it over.

Mr Victor Leverington, who was also awarded a silver Medal and certificate. was night watchman at Birmingham Market Hall during the raid that destroyed it.

Realising the helpless position of the animals at the Worcester Street end he opened the cages and liberated the kittens and fowls, ducks and rabbits, many of which were recovered and placed in crates.

Mr Leverington was assisted by Mr Edgar Garfield, who also received a silver medal and certificate. The men remained in the building until fire brigade officials instead on their going.

Mr Frank Bennett stood waist deep in a river with two frightened horses from 8am to 1pm one day.

The animals had been blown by blast out of their stables into the River Rea. Their injuries were slight, but many other horses were killed. Mr Bennett received a bronze medal and certificate.[1]

Raid 27th August 1940

Award of the British Empire Medal to Section Leader, Frank Wright, Post Office Home Guard Unit (later part of 47th Warwickshire (Birmingham G.P.O) Battalion, Royal Warwickshire Regiment). Frank Wright was commissioned as a Lieutenant on the 1st March 1942, in to the 47 Warwickshire (G.P.O) Battalion.

From the London Gazette 22nd, January 1941.

In the early hours of 27th August 1940 Section Leader Wright was on voluntary duty at Telephone House Birmingham in charge of the Home Guard detachment when a prolonged enemy air attack developed with particular intensity on the central area of the city. A number of incendiary bombs fell on and around Telephone House and started

[1] *There is another shorter account of these events in Animal World November 1940*

serious fires in the surrounding properties, most of which were completely destroyed.

During and following the attack Section Leader Wright took a leading part in the measures adopted to protect Telephone House and personally assisted in extinguishing incendiary bombs. He also organised and led an attempt to suppress the fires in adjacent properties pending the arrival of the City Fire Brigade. In addition, he took the initiative in successfully rescuing a number of Post Office motor vans from a nearby garage, which was threatened by fire from an adjacent building.

For a period of over two hours Section Leader Wright displayed courage, initiative and resource of a high order and his actions were a material contribution in saving Telephone House and Post Office property from serious damage. By his conduct throughout the incident he inspired a fine co-operative spirit in his colleagues.[1]

Raid August 1940

The award of the King's Commendation to Miss Winifred Gilhooly, a telephone operator from Castle Bromwich.

From the Birmingham Gazette September 1940
BIRMINGHAM "HELLO" GIRL COMMENDED FOR PLUCK
Among the names in the "London Gazette" of people commended for good services in connection with Civil Defence is that of Miss Winifred Gilhooly, a Birmingham telephone operator, who lives at 4, Hardware street West Bromwich.

The girl's employer considered that her conduct was worthy of the highest praise in that she carried on at the temporary exchange, which had been erected and sandbagged in the works.

It had been impossible for the usual watchman to be on duty during the night, but Miss Gilhooly, who had completed her 12 hours duty, when she knew, insisted on carrying on in charge of the telephone exchange during the night.

It was a hazardous night for bombs fell quite close; nevertheless she carried on with exemplary efficiency.[1]

Raid 26 – 27th August 1940

The award of George Medal to Engine Cleaner, Peter Frederick Smout and Examiner, Frederick Francis (Sexton) Blake, and the award of the British Empire Medal to Yard Masters Clerk, James Ernest Clarke; all being employees of the Great Western Railway.

---

[1] *Wright's commission can be found in, Home Guard List. Western Command. March 1944. 47th Warwickshire (PO) Battalion, pg. 656*

From the London Gazette 24th January 1941.

At 11pm a bomb fell in the road near a timber yard next to Bordesley Railway Yard.

Cleaner Smout, aged 17 years on hearing bombs falling left his cabin and immediately commenced dealing with incendiaries, using his hands and feet to cover them with ballast. He then volunteered to take a locomotive along the blazing goods shed, although bombs were still falling, and draw the wagons to safety. On his first journey he was accompanied on the footplate by the Depot Master's Clerk, James E Clarke but on three other trips he went alone although by this time the offside of the footplate was too hot for him to touch. Throughout the night his coolness and courage set a fine example to the other members of the railway company's staff and, but for his action, it would not have been possible to save any of the wagons lying near the burning goods shed.

Examiner Blake observed a wagon on fire and, with assistance propelled the burning vehicle to a place of safety by hand. After doing this, Blake went to the shelter and prevailed upon more of the staff to help him, He organised a squad of men and removed other burning trucks. He also acted as Shunter to Smout, and operated the point levers, which had become so hot, by using his cap. Blake afterwards put out a number of incendiary bombs using his hands and feet to cover with ballast until he found an old shovel. He then found a stirrup pump with which he extinguished the lesser fires on several trucks. Throughout the night Blake showed little regard for his own safety. By his example he led other members of the staff to help save the Company's property.

Peter Smout [1]

J.E Clarke generally supervised, did all possible to get volunteers from the shelters, assisted in removing wagons and extinguishing incendiary bombs, and moved about in all parts of the depot with total disregard for danger.

Extracts from *Heroes of Road and Rail* by George C Curnock pub 1941
CHAPTER VIII
Peter Smout
"I booked on for duty at 8.57pm. At 11 o'clock a bomb fell in the road the other side of the timber yard, smashed a gas-main, and lit up the whole yard.

It was a bit frightening at first, but I forgot it when I saw the flames from the gas-

[1] *Peter F Smout. Was from Acocks Green, and just 17 when he won his medal*

main had set the timber-yard alight, and sparks were blowing right into our big 'empties' station. This was a huge wooden shed, nearly 200 yards long and about 30 wide, with platforms from which we loaded up empty crates and packing cases, often filled with straw. Wagons ready to be loaded stood inside the shed. Others were on roads alongside. August had been very hot and dry and everything was like tinder. In no time the shed caught fire,

Frederick (Sexton) Blake
" As we went over the lines Clarke said 'There are wagons in that shed. We'll have to get them away from the fire if we can'

'We want a shunt-engine', I said. 'If we can put a road or two between them and the shed it might be enough'.

Looking for an engine we went up the sidings to the bridge, and there found one that had been left standing Clarke looked at it and saw it was under steam.

'Can you drive?' he asked me. I was about to say I'd have a try, when I saw young Smout coming across under the bridge.

'Hi, son!' I called out, seeing his loco cap, 'can you drive an engine'

'I know how' said the lad 'what do you want me to do?'

'We've got to go and fetch those wagons away from the fire' Clarke replied. He thought Smout looked too young to take on such a risky job, son added: 'If you show me how to do it, I'll drive the engine'

'I may as well do it myself,' said young Smout".

Frederick Blake [1]

Peter Smout (again)
"It was the first time I had driven an engine. I knew how, of course. My main thought was 'can I get it to do the job?'

When I got on the footplate I had to look at the gauge. The steam was down to a minimum. When an engine is left standing you've got to put it right down for fear of it blowing-off. That meant I had to get the steam up. There wasn't time to wait for it to get well up, and that was the trouble all the time.

Just at the steam was up to a point where I was ready to start a big bomb fell on the houses behind the timber-yard. I suppose it was aimed at our fire. After that I got her going.

---

[1] *Blake was a first class stoker in the Navy for 21 years. During the First World War he served on a mine sweeper, in 1920 he received a Mine Sweeper Medal for his work of clearing mines in Russian rivers.*

Blake was acting as shunter. Without him we couldn't have done the job. He had to uncouple the wagons we wanted to pull away from the burning shed and couple them up to my engine.

Our first shunt struck fast after moving a yard or so, Blake, not being a shunter in the ordinary way, hadn't realised that all the brakes would be set. When he found that out, he went all down the line releasing them.

As well as coupling and uncoupling, he had to work the points. The shed was by this time a white-hot mass of fire. Flames were blowing out over the roads where we were working. Some of the couplings were too hot to hold, so were the levers on the points nearest the fire. To make things worse, the engine hadn't enough steam up to pull a heavy load, and we had to take a few wagons at a time, which meant more journeys.

All the time we were doing this Mr Clarke[1] was helping and directing. In all, it took us a couple of hours.

Fred Blake (again)
[There were] " flames shooting up to 200 feet, making everything in the yard stand out as clear as daylight"

With Smout pushing that engine up and down [and] with myself and Clarke dodging about in the open, and everything on the move, I couldn't help but think those chaps up there in the air above us must be saying: 'Look at those shaky so-and -so's down there, running about, the bloody fools!'

My worst job was the points. Every trip Smout made, I had to shift them twice, taking the wagons off one line and putting them on another. If I'd been taller it would have been easier. I could have put more weight and leverage into it. The points swelled up with the heat and the handles got hotter and hotter. What I did was to pull my coat over my head as far as I could, take my cap in both hands, sling it over the lever, and pull for all I was worth. Smout was having a bad time with the heat, too. His footplate got so hot you couldn't touch it on the offside.

When we had been working two hours and had shifted three trains, Clarke said: 'We've done all we can. You take charge'

I went back to the bridge to have a smoke and had a quiet time until three in the morning, when Jerry let loose a lot more incendiaries. We got this lot out, and the 'All Clear' went at 4.30 am.

'What did you do?' I asked young Smout.

'The firemen had got their engine up to the shed by then' he said. 'I watched them until it was my usual time to go home'

'Did you tell your father about your engine driving?' the lad smiled in his quiet way. 'I didn't say anything. I was just as surprised, as Dad was when the notice came about my medal'

Blake was almost indignant about the recognition given to him for his share in the job.

---

[1] *James E Clarke. Was from Arden road. He was a Yardmaster Clerk at Bordesley Junction and a member of the Railway Home Guard.*

'To tell you the honest truth' he said to me. 'As I see it, I had no right to a medal. when I went up that Russian river, standing up to the middle in cold water and seeing those mines come floating down the shallows, with just one rod sticking up and tumbling about in the water – well, that was different. 300 went out on that job, and only 33 came back. We earned our silver badges all right. The King knew mine when I went up for the George, and spoke to me about it. What with the mines, and the Dover Patrol off the Belgian coast, this blitz seems pretty tame to me, and that's a fact!"

Raid 25th August, 16th October 3rd September, 18th October, 26th October 19th November 22 November and 21st December 1940, and 2nd January 1941

BEM: Edward Snape[1]
The award of the British Empire Medal to Arthur Edward Snape, Hairdresser, and War Reserve Constable.

From what appears to be the full text of a citation which was later edited for the London Gazette.

Mr Snape in addition to performing regular duty as a Special Constable has brought himself under notice by his constant attendance when air attacks have occurred. He has displayed great courage. His services as a motor driver for police work have been most useful and is a commended for his conduct in air attacks.

Sunday 9th August 1940
The first raid in which bombs were dropped in the city occurred and these bombs fell on the 'D' Division. Snape was at home, no air raid warning sirens had sounded, but on hearing explosions in the district, proceeded in his car to search the area. On arriving at Montague Road, Erdington where some houses were damaged and persons trapped. Snape entered the damaged property and assisted in the release of trapped persons and searched among debris for other possible casualties.

Thursday 13th August 1940
During air attack he was told bombs had fallen on the Castle Bromwich Aircraft Factory. He was making his way to the factory when further bombs dropped, there were numerous bomb craters and also danger from contact with machinery. He

---

[1] *A brief account of the exploits of Constable Snape appeared in the London Gazette on 11th July, 1941.*

assisted in the recovery of dead bodies, he also joined with others in a search for unexploded bombs. On many occasions Snape was obliged to fling himself to the ground for protection from flying debris, blast, splinters from gunfire etc.

Sunday 25th August 1940
High explosive bombs were dropped on the premises of the Moss Gear Co. Ltd. Chester Road and others on buildings in the district. Many unexploded bombs had also fallen. Snape assisted in searching for these, warning residents of their presence, also assisting in evacuation and the diversion of traffic.

Tuesday 3rd September 1940
Bombs fell in Tyburn Road near Constructors Ltd. One bomb fell in the garden at No 902 Tyburn Road, completely demolishing four houses and shattering the roofs and doors of other houses. Snape, whose home is very near here proceeded to evacuate people from damaged property to the Apollo Cinema nearby. Delayed action bombs had also dropped. He also obtained the assistance of four soldiers for the closing of roads.

Wednesday 16th October 1940
Whilst assisting to extinguish incendiary bombs in the Witton area, Snape fell eight feet into a hole on some allotments and although he sustained a cut and severe bruises to his left knee, and was saturated with water, he insisted in completing an eight hour tour of duty.

Friday 18th October 1940
Bombs were dropped and damage caused in the Aston district. He conveyed an Incident Officer to take up duty in Aston Road North where damage had been caused by and high explosive bomb to a shop of Messrs Wimbush Ltd. and other property. Without hesitation, he proceeded to examine the damaged property which was in a dangerous state and was able to conduct an elderly couple from a damaged upper room at one of the houses, and in spite of the continued dropping of bombs, gunfire and danger from collapsing buildings, he promptly entered the property and searched the upper floors for a child, but found only a cat whose cries had no doubt been mistaken for those of a child. He brought the cat to safety.

Friday 25th October 1940
He was returning to the Police Station for further duty when he saw a fire had started in the premises of Messrs Chaplin Bros. bedstead manufacturers 233, Park Lane, Aston – incendiaries having been dropped and immediately made his way there. Leaving his car he broke into the premises and was soon joined there by another Special Constable, and they set to work with a stirrup pump and endeavoured to

control the outbreak of fire until the arrival of the Fire Brigade . Snape then went to Aston Road North where a delayed action bomb had fallen. From eight to ten tramcars were stationary in the road, the drivers having taken shelter. Snape assisted in locating them and the tramcars were then removed from the danger area.

Saturday 26th October 1940
During an air attack a direct hit had been made upon and Anderson Shelter in Phillip Street, Aston, three people were killed and three others injured. Snape assisted on the site in the recovery of the bodies and in rescuing the injured.

Monday 26th October 1940
Bombs were dropped at the rear of houses in Aston Road North near Sutton Street. Snape was detailed to convey an Incident Officer to the scene. Having arrived, he assisted by entering several of the houses, some of which had been demolished and turned off gas at the meters in the cellar. It transpired that a delayed action bomb had also dropped here and no sooner had safety measures with regard to escaping gas been taken that the bomb exploded killing three pedestrians and injuring others.

Tuesday 19th November 1940
Incendiaries had started a fire at W H Ferris & Co., Long Acre into which high explosive bombs were being dropped. Snape gave assistance in the search of damaged houses in the vicinity for casualties, searched for a suspected unexploded bomb and helped in the evacuation of residents. It was suggested that two persons were trapped beneath debris nearby, but because of the suspected presence of an unexploded bomb the rescue party would not set to work. However, Snape took no regard for this and assisted others who volunteered for the duty, in a search of debris.

Friday 22nd November 1940
When he was near the junction of Lichfield Road and Sandy Lane, two incendiary bombs fell. Two men were making efforts to extinguish them with earth when they exploded and one of the men sustained a compound fracture of the left leg. Snape stopped his car, ran to the assistance of the man, and afterwards took the injured man in his car to the first aid post.

Saturday 21st December 1940
A paramine exploded in Alleyne road, near Wheelwright Road demolishing a shop and five houses and damaging others. It was reported that several residents were trapped. Snape was on the spot and at once assisted in a search of the damaged houses from which a few people were rescued only slightly injured. These he conveyed in his car to the first aid post. He communicated with the Report Centre

and returned to the scene and engaged in a check on the residents and ascertained that some persons were buried in the debris. He assisted in the search and using his hands removed bricks and rubble. It was necessary at times to support some of the property with timber because of the extreme danger of collapse. After continuing in this work for approximately two and half hours one woman was rescued and the body of another recovered. A paramine had also fallen and exploded in Bromford Lane, Snape also visited this scene and gave what assistance he could searching among debris, checking on residents etc.

Thursday 2nd January 1941
Snape was passing in his car along Tyburn Road, when a paramine fell and exploded at the junction of Tufnell Grove and Northleigh Road, Ward End. He made his way to the scene where there was considerable damage to houses and shops over a wide area. He assisted in a search of premises and helped with first aid to the injured, 28 of whom he conveyed in his car for further treatment at the first aid post. He remained at this scene until 5 am assisting in obtaining clothes for the residents from their damaged houses and conveying some of them to other shelter. There was heavy snow falling at the time and conditions were very bad indeed.

Raid 3rd September and 6th September 1940

The award of the George Medal to Douglas Stanley Frederick Rayner, Lieut. No 9 Bomb Disposal Company, Royal Engineers.

From the London Gazette 22nd of January 1941
On the 3rd September 1940 six unexploded bombs fell in and around an important aeroplane factory, necessitating an extensive stoppage of work. Lieutenant Rayner was on the spot within a short time, supervised the excavation of the bombs and personally removed the fuse of all six. His work was carried out so speedily that only one half day of production was lost at the factory and by his skill and courage a large portion of the works of national importance was saved from destruction.

On 6th September, 1940 in a congested factory area, Yardley a 250 kilogram (550 lb.) bomb was uncovered having a delayed action fuse. The clock was still ticking and it was realised that the danger of explosion with great damage to the factory was imminent. Fully realising the danger. Lieutenant Rayner began to withdraw the fuse, but found this had become damaged in falling and could not be moved by hand, whereupon he resorted to the use of a marlin spike and succeeded after thirty minutes in prising out the fuse. The bomb was safely removed.[1]

---

[1] *Maj. Henderson in his book Dragons Can be Defeated, gives the locations of the bombs as follows: a) Aircraft factory at Castle Bromwich, b) Factory at Yardley, Birmingham..*

Raid 6th September 1940

Award of the British Empire Medal to Lance Corporal, Edwin Charles Oxford (1920394) Royal Engineers No 9 BD Company.

From the London Gazette 22 January 1940
On 6th September 1940 an unexploded bomb fell outside a factory on priority work stopping the work there and a road leading to other important factories. Other bombs dropped at the same time in the vicinity were exploding at short intervals. Lance Corporal Oxford who was in charge of the party immediately dealt with this bomb alone rather than risk his men. The bomb was disposed of with the minimum stoppage of production. He has always been ready and willing to tackle the most dangerous points of Bomb Disposal work and had personally handled a large number of unexploded bombs.

Raid 6th September 1940
20th November and 28th November 1940

The award of the George Medal, to Sergeant, Edward Laing, 9BD Company, Royal Engineers.

London Gazette 30th September 1941
He has been engaged in bomb disposal as a Sergeant continuously since June 1940. Throughout this period (especially during the first four months, when little was known about bombs and technical equipment was non-existent) he has always shown enthusiasm for his work and complete disregard for his personal safety. He has himself carried out approximately one hundred reconnaissances and when his section was left without an officer he accepted the responsibility of Section Officer with quiet success.

Incident: 'A' - September 1940, Birmingham
A 250 kilogram bomb fell on the Ryvita Factory and penetrated to a depth of thirty two feet beneath the foundations of a main wall. During excavations a strata of old calcium carbide was encountered at a depth of seventeen feet. One man was overcome by fumes in the hole and extracted at great personal risk by the N.C.O who personally went into the hole and cleared out the remaining carbide, thus enabling work to continue. Owing to restricted excavation, when the bomb was finally reached, it could only be recovered by Sergeant Laing himself, lying flat on the bomb, and using a trowel to gain access to the fuses.

Incident: 'B' - November 20th 1940   G.E.C. Works, Witton, Birmingham.
    28th November 1940   B.S.A. (Guns), Birmingham

The above bombs, both 250-kilogram, were dropped at 20.30 and 23.00 hours respectively. He took charge of the parties which commenced work within four and a half and three hours respectively and by energy, initiative and steadiness, the bombs were safely removed.

Raid 15th October and 25th October 1940

The award of the British Empire Medal to Miss Winifred Yate (ARP Warden)

From: the London Gazette 13th June 1941

During August, September, October and November 1940, a number of Air raids, occurred on this city and on each occasion Miss Winifred Yate, 35 Gopsal Street, a voluntary warden reported for duty on the sounding of the sirens and immediately went out on the Sector and patrolled whether or not bombs were falling and during anti-aircraft fire.

Whilst patrolling she was instrumental in locating at least 6 incidents, where either H.E or incendiary bombs had fallen, and also reported the particulars to the Report Centre, afterwards returning to the scenes and assisted in extinguishing a number of incendiary bombs.

On Tuesday 15th October 1940 at about 23.30 hours incendiary bombs were dropped and caused a major fire in the Goods Sheds at Curzon Street, L.M.&S Railway. Miss Yate ran to the nearest wardens Post, which is situated at her home about 200 yards away from the scene and reported the incident to the Fire Brigade and found that it was necessary to evacuate about 200 horses, owned by the Railway Company, from stables adjoining the fire. The horses were released from the stables and Miss Yate gave great assistance in leading two horses at a time to stables about a quarter of a mile away. These horses are the very heavy cart horses and are the Belgian type, being very

Miss Winifred Yate [1]

---

[1] *Photograph of Miss Yate from the Birmingham Gazette, Saturday 14th June, 1941.*

timid at fire. Whilst the horses were being led away, bombs were dropping in the vicinity and there was heavy anti-aircraft fire. On this night Miss Yate lost her steel helmet and carried on throughout the raid without protection. She remained at the scene giving all the assistance she could until the Raiders Passed sounded.

On 25th October 1940, rescued two men from fallen debris in Ashted Row, and rendered first aid to the injured, and was herself injured by a bomb explosion.

She has performed meritorious service, marked by gallantry and devotion to duty, and is now recommended for recognition.

Raid 15th to 16th October 1940

The award of the George Cross, to Section Commander, George Walter Inwood[1] and British Empire Medal to, Leonard Isoyn Tidball Volunteer both of the 10th Birmingham Battalion. Home Guard. British Empire Medal to Police Inspector William Frank Wade (for this incident and others), George Medal to Edwin John Woodland, Depot Superintendent; George Medal to Harold Rainbow, Forman and Lewis Pickersgill, Second Man (all members of the ARP Rescue Party Kingston Wharf Depot.

The air raid warning was sounded at 8.07pm on Tuesday 15th October and at 8.40 p.m. bombs commenced to fall on this "A" Division. One high explosive bomb struck and demolished three dwelling houses and a small factory, numbers 141 to 143 Bishop Street, trapping a number of residents who had taken refuge beneath these houses in a strengthened shelter made out of the cellars. Police Inspector William Frank Wade immediately set up an incident Post, at Messrs Weathershields,

Bishop Street. Inspector Wade sent for rescue and First Aid Squads. In addition to the bombing continuing an escape of gas of a severe nature from a fractured main hampered the rescue workers. This escape of gas was reported and frequent requests were made for gas workers and equipment to be sent. At 9.37 p.m. two men were rescued alive and at 10.28 p.m. a boy was brought from the wreckage and found to be dead. A hole was made in the debris and efforts were made to rescue the trapped persons who could be heard calling. One man's body could be seen. Inspector Wade tried to get down the hole but failed as he was too big, but he was able to assist by lying on his stomach and assist the man in the hole by throwing out debris.

At 10.56 p.m. Inspector Wade was pulled away

Inspector Wade

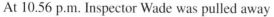

---

[1] *There are additional accounts of the actions of George Inwood in The Times, 28th May 1941; Birmingham Evening Despatch, 28th May 1941; Birmingham Gazette, 28th May 1941.*

from the hole which was full of coal gas, by Special constable Pare, he went to his incident post and recovered after vomiting, then he returned to the hole. Section Commander Inwood was called upon by the police to help in the rescue duty. Taking charge of a party of six volunteers, he found several people were imprisoned in the gas filled cellar. Section commander Inwood was lowered into the cavity and with great bravery he succeeded in bringing up two males alive. Though near exhausted, he entered the cavern a third time and was overcome by fumes. He was dragged out by one of his comrades, Volunteer L.I. Tidball, Home Guard, but despite the attention of a doctor and nurse it was impossible to revive him, and he died at 11.53pm. He showed the highest form of cool courage and self sacrifice for others. Tidball too was overcome by fumes but recovered in hospital.

During this time extensive bombing was going on at short intervals, the enemy being guided to the district by incendiary fires started in the districts of Rea Street and Digbeth. Volunteers were again called for to enter the cellar as it was thought there was still a possibility that some of the people trapped were alive. Knowing that Inwood had previously made the attempt and had died, Pickersgill, Woodland and Rainbow volunteered. Pickersgill entered the cellar first and was overcome. Woodland then entered and rescued Pickersgill. He also brought another body to the entrance. Woodland, himself, was then overcome. At this stage, Rainbow entered and rescued Woodland. All three were rendered unconscious and two were transported to hospital[1].

Left - H. Rainbow, Right - L. Pickersgill

[1] *A fuller account of the incident is included in the recommendation for the BEM of Constable Wade.*

In respect of Woodland, Rainbow and Pickersgill, Official records at the Public Records Office show their date of incident as 10th October 1940. This date appears to be an error and is not supported by other evidence. There is no record of a raid near Bishop Street on the 10th and the death of Inwood is confirmed on the Birmingham Hospital Contributory Association, Emergency Hospital Scheme -Information for Relatives, Fatal Casualties List and other sources.

George Walter Inwood G.C. is buried in grave 46739, Yardley Cemetery Birmingham. Special Constable Pare was awarded £1.1s.0d by the Watch Committee for his service at the incident. Inspector Wade was awarded the BEM for this incident, and also for service during air raids during August, October, November and December 1940. Sadly, Edmund Pickersgill committed suicide in 1955, following a breakdown in his health as a result of his war service; he was only 48[1].

Headstone of George Walter Inwood

26th October 1940

The award of the, King's Commendation, to Mrs Julia Pearson, of the Post Office, whilst working as part of the A.R.P Casualty Service, First Aid Post, Kent Street Baths.

London Gazette, 21st March 1941
Official recommendation; Mrs Pearson of 66 Bristol Road, should be commended for her gallantry. It was recorded that she was in fact herself struck by a piece of projectile which broke the metal button off her steel helmet. She showed the greatest coolness and steadiness in issuing orders and in dealing personally with the casualties.

From City Under Siege Part IV, Birmingham Evening Mail supplement.
At 9.50 p.m. a high explosive bomb crashed through the circular skylight of the baths and exploded near the staircase, leading to the basement.

Shortly before, Mrs. Julia Pearson, the First Aid Post's officer, had ordered staff to shelter in the basement and all but three Miss I Brooks, Miss D Adams and Mrs

---

[1] *Evening Mail, 21st September, 1955.*

C Lyson took cover. When the bomb exploded Mrs Pearson was manning the telephone in the post's office. The glass partition shattered and she was bruised and cut but carried on working and kept control of the situation.

Three people were killed outright by the explosion, Miss Adams, a Mr Lewis and the baths attendant, Mr H Rose. Others were seriously injured and two later died in hospital.

Raid 26th October 1940.

The award of the British Empire Medal, to Police Constable C,114 Leslie Thomas, Brearley Street/ Summer Lane.

London Gazette, 14th March 1941.

During an air raid, Constable Thomas was posted to protection duty on 26th October, 1940 outside the works of Newey Bros., Brearley Street, whose premises consist of two buildings, viz. the main block at the corner of Summer Lane and Brearley Street, and a smaller building in Brearley Street, about 50 yards away. At about 8.50p.m. incendiary bombs were dropped in large numbers in the neighbourhood, and fires were started. Thomas telephoned to Bridge Street West Police Station asking for the assistance of the fire services, and he then commenced to deal himself with the bombs and fires.

He dealt with two bombs which had fallen in the street, and with the aid of Mr Benwell, a civilian, put out two others in Hatchett Street, by covering them with sand obtained from sand bags outside premises. He then saw that another bomb had set fire to a shed at Messrs Newey's branch works. With the aid of Mr Benwell, the yard doors were burst open and with the assistance of members of the firms Home Guard, packing cases were removed from the shed and the fire was put out with a stirrup pump. On reaching the street the Constable found that an incendiary bomb had set fire to the top floor of the premises of Messrs Witton, Woodturners, Brearley Street. These premises contained a large quantity of timber and inflammable material used in the manufacture of furniture. He endeavoured to borrow fire appliances from Newey's, but they were all in use in extinguishing other fires in their premises so he forced an entrance into Witton's premises and went to the polishing room on the top floor where the fire was burning fiercely. One incendiary bomb was hanging from the roof and another had fallen into a vessel in the middle of the room near to where a quantity of spirit stain was placed. There was no water in the room, so the Constable returned downstairs, found water and buckets, and with the assistance of members of Newey's Home Guard formed a chain of persons carrying water, and attacked the fire. He removed the spirit stain and eventually put out the fire.

Constable Thomas was then informed that another fire had commenced in the premises of Messrs Ward's, Brearley Street, the incendiary bomb having penetrated the roof, second and first floors, causing smouldering woodwork on each floor. When he again reached the street Thomas saw that a fresh fire had broken out in the branch of Newey's on the first floor. He went there and with the help of one of their Home Guards he forced an entrance to the premises and extinguished the fire. He then saw that the timber yard of Messrs Raven, Brearley Street, were on fire, burning furiously and realising that this fire might endanger the safety of persons in a public shelter in Hatchett Street, at the rear of the premises he arranged for their removal to another shelter.

During the whole time that Police Constable was engaged in dealing with the fires, enemy air attacks were continuing on the city and planes were overhead, and over a dozen high explosive bombs were dropped in the neighbourhood. As the district where he had been working was lighted up by the fires, he was in great danger from falling bombs. He was wet through, covered with dirt and grime and almost on the point of exhaustion when relieved. There is no doubt that by his prompt action in dealing with the fires at Witton's premises and Newey's works, he saved the premises from total destruction, which would have resulted in important work being held up[1].

Raid October 1940

Award of King's Commendation to Alfred Jervis (Hotel House Porter)

London Gazette 7th February 1941
Was employed at the Heathfield Hotel, Moseley. In October 1940, with the aid of a ladder, he forced an entrance into the upper floor of a building and extinguished a fire. Afterwards, single-handed, he dealt with other incendiaries, which fell in the neighbourhood.

October 1940

Award of Military Medal to 1442084 Bombardier (fitter) Horace Charles Bradley Royal Artillery.

London Gazette 27th December 1941.
H.C Bradley was stationed at a site, which was continually attacked by high explosive and incendiary bombs. During a heavy night raid on Birmingham he carried a wounded comrade to a place of safety and fought a number of fires. During the attack, in which three men were killed and seven wounded, fires were started. Bradley showed great courage and initiative and throughout the night his energy and coolness in the performance of his duty were a splendid example to all.[2]

---

[1] *There is a picture of Constable Thomas receiving has award in the, Birmingham Gazette,*
[2] *Story also appeared in the Birmingham Gazette 27th Dec 1941.*

15th and 29th October and 4th December 1940 10th April and 17th May 1941.

Award of the George Medal to Dr Halstead Middleton Turnbull M.R.C.S L.R.C.P Major 31st (Birmingham) Battalion Royal Warwickshire Regiment (Home Guard)

Extract from recommendation of commendation.

Dr Turnbull, as one of two medical officers (the other was a Dr Griffiths) working in the first aid rooms attached to Rowton House, Alcester Street, gave most valuable help and steadiness to the 600 occupants of Rowton House at a time when a direct hit by an enemy bomb caused a number of casualties on 15th October, 1940. On 29th October and 4th December, 1940 Dr Turnbull gave similar courageous care to casualties brought to the first aid rooms at Rowton House at a time when these rooms had just been badly damaged by blast. He is reported to have shown the coolest of courage and resourcefulness in dealing with the situation, with total disregard to his own personal safety. On April 10th, 1941 at houses I Birchall Street, Ravenshurst Street and Vaughton Street, Highgate he made strong endeavours, though unsuccessfully, to enter a cellar blocked with debris during a raid, in order to assist persons trapped in the cellar. At the same time he dealt with a number of serious casualties on the spot. In relation to the same raid, Dr Turnbull attended a women recently confined, who was unable to leave her house, giving her treatment and sitting by her until an ambulance arrived, although this and other houses had been compulsorily evacuated by reason of the presence of delayed action bomb. During a raid on May 17th 1941 at a house in Artillery Street, Bordesley, Dr Turnbull made his way head first down a narrow opening into a basement of the house blocked with debris, the wall being in danger of collapsing in order to give morphia to an injured casualty. He then assisted to remove debris and dealt with casualties as they were brought out.[1]

Amelia Johnson B.E.M assisted Dr Turnbull in Ravenshurst Street.

Maj. H. M. Turnbull

[1] *Dr Turnbull died at the age of 68, in 1970. Report in the Birmingham Mail 24th Aug 1970.*

Raid 17th October 1940

The award of the British Empire Medal to Walter Samuel Garvey, A.R.P Warden. British Empire Medal to Harry Goodwin, A.R.P Warden. British Empire Medal Stanley Charles Green, Auxiliary Fireman.

London Gazette 25th April 1941.
At about 8.10p.m a high explosive bomb struck numbers 207, 209 and 211 Knowle Road, Sparkhill completely demolishing the houses. Numbers 205 and 213 were also severely damaged. Mr and Mrs Ellis at 205 were trapped in the pantry by debris and Goodwin accompanied by Green of the A.F.S and Warden Garvey climbed over the debris and succeeded in rescuing them. This was done at great risk to themselves owing to the conditions of the property. Mr and Mrs Parton, their baby aged two years, Mr Parton's brother and Mrs Hyde were trapped beneath the debris in number 213. The houses were in a dangerous condition, but Goodwin, Garvey and Green worked continuously for about three hours, although the roof under which they were working was in danger of collapse. The raid continued, but at no time did they take shelter. The men found the position of the women and her child and first rescued the child, sending it at once to the First Aid Post. Then Mrs Parton was eventually got out and sent away to an ambulance. One of the rescuers got into the hole which had been made near the woman, held up the debris and talked to her whilst the work was in progress. The other three persons lost their lives, their bodies being found the following day.

Harry Goodwin

The following report appeared in the Birmingham Gazette 26th April 1941.
Three Hour Fight to Save Woman.

Four Birmingham men are in the first list of winners of the British Empire Medal (Civil Division) which, as announced on Tuesday, takes the place of the medal of the O.B.E in recognising air raid gallantry, but is of higher value.

Three of the Birmingham winners of the medal, Walter Samuel Garvey and Harry Goodwin A.R.P Wardens and Stanley Charles Green, Birmingham A.F.S – worked together to rescue four trapped people during a heavy raid.

Birmingham Evening Despatch 29th April 1941 (pg. 3)

Behind the recent announcement that Harry Goodwin of 164 Knowle Road, Sparkhill, Birmingham had been awarded the British Empire Medal, lies the story of a 32 year old carpenter and joiner, who cannot decide whether to become a handicrafts teacher or to go on repairing the damaged homes of poor people.

He started his career as a cabinet trade apprentice and carefully saved every penny towards starting up in business himself. Now his efforts have been rewarded and he has plenty of government orders for ladders.

If needed he puts in many mornings working on houses damaged by bomb. Mr Goodwin joined the A.R.P as Divisional Warden early in 1938 and went through all his first aid and gas tests.

Now that his work takes up so much of his time he is patrolling warden on duty where there is a raid etc.

17th October 1940

The award of the King's Commendation to Leonard Allen, (Blacksmith); Alan Henry Harden, (Machinist); Kenneth Thomas Roger, (Clerk) Leslie Michael McSweeney (Police Constable D. 138); and George Charles Henry Matthews, (Police Constable D64).

London Gazette 14th March 1941

Commendations for courageous conduct during an air attack. No venue given but understood to have been in the Stechford area of the City.

Raids on 27th August and 18th October 1940

Award of the British Empire Medal to Horace Edward Jones, (Forman Carpenter) and the King's Commendation to Arthur Enoch Hudson, (Carpenter and Joiner) and Robert Porter, (Works Maintenance Engineer)
London Gazette 13th June 1941

A rescue squad under the leadership of Horace E. Jones was sent to an incident and found the house in a state of collapse.

The victims at the above job were trapped under the staircase which had collapsed under the weight of debris and Jones immediately made a hole in the debris despite falling brickwork and with great difficulty cut through the staircase to find seven people trapped underneath three children and four adults. Whilst engaged on this the front of the house collapsed. The children and two adults were extracted alive one of them a male, was badly trapped by the legs one of which was broken. Jones freed this man and placed splints upon the broken leg. During this operation a delayed action bomb fell in the garden 50 yards away but Jones and his men continued to work throughout the night. At one period the men had forcibly removed Jones from his work as he was in a state of exhaustion but he quickly recovered and resumed work until the other two victims were recovered. This was an outstanding piece of gallantry for during the whole time incendiary and High Explosive bombs were falling in the district.

At 88; 90 and 92 Gough Road Edgbaston Birmingham on October 18th 1940 these men were members of a party of rescue men who made a gallant but unavailing attempt to tunnel through the cellar of one house in an attempt to get at five persons who were trapped in the cellar of the house adjoining. This was an outstanding piece of gallantry, for during the whole time the walls of the cellar and the floors over were collapsing under the strain of the debris load on top. After several attempts had been abandoned Jones, assisted by one of his men S Purton again entered this particular portion of the cellar and made a great effort to prop and support the collapsing walls and ceiling, but their attempts were in vain. Hudson at great risk succeeded in cutting a hole through the party walls for the cellar and thus enabled the victims to obtain air.[1]

19th October, 12 December 1940
and 10th April 1941

Award of the George Medal to Thomas Henry Sharman, Captain (71764) 9th Bomb Disposal Unit. Royal Engineers.

London Gazette 30th September 1941
He has been engaged continuously on bomb disposal duties since June 1940. As a section Officer during that period he has extracted approximately two hundred bombs and has carried out the same number of reconnaissances. On at least four occasions he has escaped, by minutes, bombs which spontaneously exploded when being reconnoitred.
Incident "A" 19th Oct 1940.
At 00.30 hours the party were on the Category "A" bomb at the G.E.C Works Witton, when a heavy raid was in progress. The bomb, which had been down for only two and a half-hours, was found to be a 250-Kilogram bomb with a (17) fuse, which was successfully extracted by 09.30 hours the same day.

Incident "B" 12th Dec 1940.
A report was received at 01.30 hours that a bomb had fallen at the B.S.A (Guns) Factory, Small Heath. He took a party to the site but found that the wrong location had been given. Despite the fact that a very heavy raid was in progress, he continued to search and eventually located a 250-Kilogram bomb as B.S.A (Tools) Factory some two miles away. He commenced work at 03.00 hours and worked continuously

---

[1] *Horace Edward Jones, 42 Runcorn Rd, Bham; Arthur Hudson, 39 Lincoln Street, Balsall Heath and Robert Porter, 21 Jakeman Rd, Bham.*

until 14.00 hours on 14th December when the (17) fuse was successfully withdrawn. During the night of 13th December, another heavy raid took place and many bombs fell in the area.

Incident "C" 10th April 1941
He dealt successfully with a Category "A" bomb at Wolseley Motors Factory, Small Heath. The bomb was diagnosed as a 250 kilogram containing both (17) and (50) fuses, but, as a result of the officer's determination, it was safely removed fourteen hours after it fell. Vital work was not interrupted.

Raid 22nd October 1940

The award of the George Medal to William Shutt (Insurance Agent) Auxiliary Fireman.

London Gazette 14th March 1941
On the night of October 22nd 1940, at about midnight, Sub-Officer Shelldrake was placed in charge of a large fire with several crews under his control. The buildings affected were some six old fashioned factories. Most of the buildings were apparently of the four-storey nature, and in the centre of this group of buildings was a courtyard. The whole area affected was about 10,000 square yards.

After about one hour little progress could be made owing to three gas mains which were burning at various parts of the fire. Apart from encouraging the fire the gas mains created a vivid light which would naturally attract the attention of enemy raiders.

Auxiliary Shutt volunteered to enter the buildings and attempt to cut off the gas at the various points. Under extremely dangerous conditions in which apart from the fire, heavy girders, machinery and walls were continually falling, he worked in the building for about 40 minutes when he was finally brought out against his will in an exhausted condition by Sub-Officer Shelldrake. He advanced through the blazing buildings across the small courtyard to points about 80 yards for the road. However, he was

William Shutt

only successful in partially reducing the gas jets in two instances as soon as he was in the roadway he insisted on working at the gas turn-cock in the street pavement, and although the necessary appliances were not available he, with the help of the others eventually turned off the gas main after about three quarters of an hour's work.[1]

Raid 24th October 1940

The award of the King's Commendation, to Police Constable C.268 Charles Manners, probationary constable.

London Gazette 7th/3rd/1941
Commendations for courageous conduct during an air attack, in Cox Street, off Livery Street[1].

Date Unknown

The award of the British Empire Medal to Walter Taylor, Voluntary Fireman, Bulpitt & Sons Ltd.

London Gazette 3rd /1st/1941
When a fire was started by enemy attack at some works, Fireman Taylor showed great courage in going into a burning building, part of which had fallen in, to attack the heart of a fire which threatened to destroy the works. He was not at the time on duty with the Auxiliary Fire Service (A.F.S) or at the works. His brave action saved a section of the building.

Raid 26th October 1940

The award of the George Medal to A.R.P Warden Frederick Parkes

London Gazette 12th /12th/1940
Parkes who was not on duty heard that a bomb had been dropped on some works, Rowlands Electrical Accessories Ltd., (Hockley Hill) and he immediately went to see if he could be of assistance. A high explosive bomb had been dropped close to the outside wall and the premises were well alight as a three-inch gas main had been broken and the gas ignited. The works roof watchers had been able to get down from these works. Mr Parkes went into the premises to see if it was possible to extinguish the fire. A considerable quantity of sand was applied to the source of the blaze but this was found to be ineffective. They then stopped an A.F.S tender and the leader of the squad and Parkes made their way as far along the passage entrance as the could,

---

[1] *The premises involved was the Jubilee Works, Buckingham Street. Photo of Mr Shutt and letter in Minton Collection.*

but it was decided that it was impossible to get into the building, as there was every likelihood of the remaining unfallen structure coming down. Parkes was aware of the exact position of the gas cock in the cellar of the adjacent premises, and with the assistance of another employee managed to enter the cellar, head first through a small opening of 12 inches to 15 inches square, and turn off the gas at the main. The fire was then extinguished without much difficulty. His action, a particularly courageous one, undoubtedly saved the whole of these works from destruction.

Frederick Parkes - Birmingham Gazette 1944

From Birmingham Gazette 18th/11th/1944

V.C.s Meet G.M Who Saved Works in Raid

Continuing their tour of Birmingham and District works connected in the manufacture of the PIAT Mortar and bombs were at the 12th works visited by them during the week; and here they met Mr F. Parkes G.M. of 46 Robert Road, Handsworth, a senior charge hand employed by the firm.

As was explained by the governing director of the firm. This meeting between the V.C.s and the G.M. could not have taken place in that building, but for the action of Mr Parkes on 26th October 1940, when, as a warden in the work's A.R.P organisation, he won his George Medal

The premises were on fire as a result of a hit during an enemy raid, the high-pressure gas main was alight. Although Mr Parkes need not have been on duty – it was his night off – he was lowered head first into the cellar, crawled under the burning building and turned off the gas at the main, so that the fire-engine were able to get the outbreak under control and extinguished it.[1]

Raid 25th/26th October 1940

The award of the George Medal to Alfred Leslie Holford, works Foreman/Chargehand, Fremo Works Moseley Street.

London Gazette 17th /1st/1941

For courage and resource under enemy air attack.

At nightfall on October 25th, 1940 the enemy dropped a large salvo of incendiary

---

[1] *There is a photo of Mr Parkes in the Birmingham Gazette, 18/11/1944, page 2.*

bombs on Birmingham, setting on fire the premises of Messrs. Harcourt near those of Mountfords. On his own initiative, Holford, a Foreman/Chargehand, at once attacked the fire on these premises with his own firm's fire pump. After some time it was found that the premises of another firm, adjoining, were on fire and flames were threatening these buildings. At once he tackled the new blaze and for two hours worked alone, in great difficulties as the only means of approach for houses lay over long lengths of roof. He went on, in spite of enemy aircraft, which were still about. The fire was mastered and confined to Harcourt's premises.

Some hours later, two further attacks set a third factory ablaze. Firemen were in a very perilous position on the roof and with the probability that large stocks of highly explosive materials in burning buildings might, at any time, explode, by his tenacity and courage saved his factory. He refused to leave until 06.00, when he handed over to the regular Fire Brigade.

Raid 25th /26th October 1940

The award of the British Empire Medal to Jack Reynolds, A.R.P Messenger, Casual Labourer.

London Gazette 12th /12th/1941

During an air raid on the night of the, 26th October, 1940, a house at 163 Brighton Road was demolished by an high explosive bomb, six occupants being trapped in the cellar. At the risk of great personal danger from falling debris and structural collapse Reynolds volunteered to crawl along the beams and enter the cellar by means of a very small aperture. He succeeded in rescuing three injured and one uninjured person, and then reported that there were two who were too heavy for him to move. A rope was passed to him and a sheet of iron. He tied the rope round the people's waists and, using the sheet of iron as a slide, these two were drawn up through the aperture. Undoubtedly, the boy's heroism has saved these persons lives.

Raid 26th October 1940

The award of the George Medal to Platoon Officer R.E. Cooke, Auxiliary Bomb Disposal Squad, and Second Lieutenant R.H. Lee 9th Bomb Disposal Company, Royal Engineers.

From *"Designed to Kill"* By Mason Arthur Hogben

One of the first members of the Home Guard to be awarded a decoration for work in bomb disposal was Platoon Officer R.E. Cooke, a member of an auxiliary bomb disposal squad of Messrs Burman Ltd, at Leebank Works, Highland Road, Birmingham. On 26 October 1940 a 250 kg (550 lb) bomb fell on the machine shop of Messrs Burman and failed to explode. The factory at that time was engaged on vital aircraft production work and so the bomb was given a high priority for clearance and a Royal Engineer detachment form 9 Bomb Disposal Company, R.E under the command of Second Lieutenant R.H. Lee, was detailed to clear it. Despite the combined efforts of the Army and the auxiliary squad the bomb was not exposed until 28th October 1940, some 45 hours after it had fallen. Upon inspection it was found to have a clockwork long delay fuse which was still ticking. In view of the time, which had elapsed since the bomb had fallen, its detonation was probable at any moment. Second Lieutenant Lee cleared his men and the members of the auxiliary squad for the area and attempted unsuccessfully to remove the fuse. After fifteen minutes determined work he had to admit defeat and withdrew to consider the next move. In view of the importance of the factory it was decided to attack the fuse a second time but with less finesse and more brute force. (The fuse would be prized out with a crowbar!) This could not be done by one person alone and Mr Cook volunteered to assist. At this attempt they managed to break off the top of the fuse but the dangerous clockwork mechanism was still ticking and the bomb's detonation was imminent. It was then decided to flood the hole in which the bomb was lying in an endeavour to stop the clock. Second Lieutenant Lee and Mr Cooke completed this task together and to their relief the clock stopped and the bomb was safely removed. Both Second Lieutenant Lee and Platoon Officer Cooke were subsequently awarded George Medals.

From a personal account by R. Mackeryie.

I was in charge of the Sunday Firecrew (Messrs Burman Ltd) and the raid Saturday had been around the Bristol Road area and the logbook reported a bang around the old works. Bomb Disposal had been called and they concluded that a small, twenty kg or so bomb had come through and exploded doing no damage. I went over and there was a hole in the old toolroom roof, and a smaller hole in the floor, right by George Phillips cutter grinder, and in the ground floor by the old handling shop there was a large crack and a small casting grinding machine was tipped up a few degrees. Monday morning Tommy F was put to work to reset the casting grinder and after moving the machine, started to break away the concrete around the crack to relay out, as he went deeper the crack got wider and when he was into the bubble it developed into a large hole until finally he had a pit some six feet deep and almost as square. He was merrily *bashing* away with his pickaxe when he heard a metallic clang as the pick hit something, so he scraped away the loose earth and there was a rather large bomb which after the belt with the pick had started to tick. This information ran round the works like wildfire "evacuate".

In three minutes flat the place was deserted, except for Home Guard and Fire Service personnel, who could be caught to guard the barriers, set up around Lee Bank, Bell Barn etc and the bomb disposal men were fetched back. They weren't sure about the fuses so the hole was flooded and sandbagged and they cheerfully said "if it has not exploded by 6 o'clock it will be safe to move" so every one sweated blood all night including Sir Charles, who kept us supplied with fish and chips and fags as usual and kept looking in the hole. At precisely 6am bomb disposal came back and removed the bomb. I think it was just turned 8 o'clock when it was taken off to the Garrison Lane Dump, where I believe it exploded five minutes after it got there; whether deliberately or not I don't know.

Raid 26th / 27th October 1940

The award of the George Medal to, Section Leader, Alfred Henry George Brunges and, Patrol Leader, Charles William Lovelace Tozer; 2nd Birmingham Battalion, Home Guard.[1]

From London Gazette 30/09/1941

A bomb demolished a public shelter. Patrol Leader Tozer and Section Leader Brunges showed the utmost bravery and devotion to duty in voluntarily going to the aid of a considerable number of persons who were trapped. The explosion had blown in the outer wall of the basement shelter, causing the collapse of one end of the specially prepared structure, the remainder of the building had completely caved in, both the gas main and water pipe had burst.

Brunges and Tozer endeavoured to gain access form the main entrance to the basement, which was completely blocked, and this was accomplished after difficulty, working in the dark.

The basement was filling rapidly with water, people who were trapped were buried under piles of debris, or held down by parts of the structure and working space was extremely limited. The work of rescue could be carried out only by taking the risk of moving loose beams and this was highly dangerous owing to huge blocks of concrete form the floor above being dislodged. The two men took the risk without a moment's thought of their own safety.

The removal of the debris form those buried had to be done with their hands, mostly under water and in kneeling or half lying position. The work was carried on for nearly four hours until twenty people had been removed.[2]

Section Leader A H G Brunges

---

[1] *Pictures of both recipients appear in the history of the Birmingham Home Guard Battalions.*
[2] *Reports of the award also appeared in the, Times, 01/10/1941 and the, Birmingham Mail, 01/10/1941.*

Letter to Mike Minton from Alfred Brunges, 1983.

Q Is there anything specific you remember about the incident.

A Quite a lot, most of which I would like to forget. I received no papers whatever from London. It all (the George Medal) came through our Captain. I have read that a Fruit and Veg shop owned by Mr Willetts was involved but this is not so. It was the 'Public Shelter' at the corner of Basken St Lozells, opposite the Villa Cross picture house that it happened.

Letter to Mike Minton from Charles Tozer, 1983

I am Charles William Lovelace Tozer G.M. and the details you asked for are as follows: -

Bonner Hall, Hunters Rd, Birmingham was our Home Guard H.Q. From there we would go out and help the public in any way we could during Air Raids; we also helped the police. My wife was evacuated, and so I had more time to spend at H.Q. On the 27th of October 1940 a bomb was dropped about a hundred yards from H.Q. and landed on Willets Fruit shop, which had a 'Public Shelter' below it; it was a direct hit.

I ran with one of my men to the shelter, the tram cable post was down, and cable was on the road and the shelter, or what was left of it was. A young women was on top of the shelter debris, I clambered in and got her out, then handed her to the man with me, he took her to Bonner Hall.

Several people were trapped under the debris and I could hear some of them. It seemed hopeless to get them out as the basement was filling with water, the gas main had been broken and electricity cable was everywhere. Then I heard a child crying and somehow I crawled through a mass of beams and debris. I got to the child who was crying, but having no light I could not see the extent of the injury, however I was able to lift him. Just then a large block of concrete fell and blocked my way out.

I had been in this shelter before and had seen some stone steps at the entrance. I made my way through the debris, in this

Charles Tozer

direction taking the child with me; there were a number of people, which I passed, who were all either injured or dead. As I got to the steps Brunges was making a hole at the top and was able to pull the child through. The water seemed to get no worse and the gas eased off and so I was able to go back time and again, first getting the live ones out and then the dead.

Brunges, was working from the other side doing the same. Someone had provided a light and people at the top of the steps had cleared the hole and so I was able to see more clearly: the worst part was the children. I was in the shelter about two hours and there were only a few dead, that we could not get, that were left.

I was a skilled man and had been turned down from the Forces because of this, but in that shelter I made a vow that some how I would get into the Forces and kill every German I could get near enough to. I changed from a nice fellow to a bitter one, who needed revenge, as I was only young and I thought this way. Eventually I got into the Army and became a Sergeant Major, but that's another story.

Raids 18th October till 11th December 1940

Award of the British Empire Medal to Special Constable Emmanuel Graham (Managing director of a catering and confectionery company)

London Gazette 20th /6th / 1941
18/10/40. Gough Road, Edgbaston. Two houses demolished by H.E. bombs five people trapped by falling debris.

On this occasion Special Constable Graham was not actually on duty, but on hearing the sirens sounding, immediately drove to Ladywood Police Station, and offered his services. He was instructed to convey two constables in his motor car to the above incident, and during the journey bombs were falling in the vicinity. On arrival at the incident it was found that two houses had been demolished and five people were trapped beneath the debris. S.C Graham assisted the Rescue Squad in removing the debris, and was thus engaged until 5 a.m.

28/10/40. Bristol Street and vicinity. Serious fires cased by incendiary bombs.
S.C. Graham was on Reserve Duty at Ladywood Police Station. He was instructed to convey Constables to incidents in Bristol Street and Bristol Road areas where H.E bombs and incendiaries had fallen. Craters and debris were strewn about the roads through which he had to drive his motor car. During this time H.E. bombs and incendiaries were still falling. He then went to Bristol Street Police Station and asked for further instructions. He was then ordered to take Constables to Pershore Road where H.E. bombs had fallen. This he did driving through streets which were lined by burning buildings. After this he returned to Bristol Street Station. Buildings in the vicinity were on fire and it became necessary to remove persons from the fire

danger zone. Whilst removing these persons debris had fallen, and frequently he found streets impassable owing to burning buildings and craters, and this necessitated him finding another route. He persevered in his efforts, however, and was successful in getting his passengers to safety.

5/11/40. Oozells Street, Ladywood. Messrs. Wales Ltd. Bedding premises, hit by oil bomb; and other incidents in Stoke Street and vicinity.

S.C. Graham was on Reserve Duty at Ladywood Police Station, and was instructed to convey Constables to the premises of Messrs. Wales Ltd. Oozells Street, which had been hit by and oil bomb and was on fire. He returned to Ladywood and was then instructed to take officers to Stoke Street where H.E. bombs had fallen and which on their journey his car was struck by shrapnel. On arrival at the scene of the incident he assisted in releasing trapped persons from an air raid shelter. After this he returned to Oozells Street, assisting in the direction of traffic.

22/11/40 Monument Road area comprising, Kenilworth Court, Hagley Road, Edgbaston Cinema, Monument Road, Bellis Street, Waterworks Road, and Reservoir Road.

On this occasion S.C. Graham was at his business premises in Monument Road when a number of H.E. bombs fell in this district. He left his premises and walked to Bellis Street where H.E. bombs had fallen demolishing houses; organised search parties for injured persons; established an incident post at his own premises, and telephoned to Ladywood police station giving details, and arranged for the necessary services to be sent. S.C. Graham then went to an incident in Waterworks Road, where a dwelling house had been demolished and others had been damaged. He rendered all the assistance he could, found that gas was escaping from the main and telephoned for the gas services to be sent. He remained at the scene of this incident until relieved by the regular police, and then got out his motor car, drove to Ladywood Police Station and reported for duty, where he was engaged in taking Police Officers to other incidents until 6 a.m. next morning.

Special Con. Graham [1]

11/12/40. Carpenter Road, Edgbaston. Two D.A. bombs.

S.C. Graham was on duty at Ladywood Police Station when it was reported that delayed action bombs had fallen in Carpenter Road. He was instructed to convey Police Officers to the scene. On arrival he assisted in searching for the D.A. bombs

[1] *Picture of Special Constable Graham appeared in the, Birmingham Gazette, 21.6.1941.*

and was successful in locating one of them. During this time H.E. bombs were falling in the vicinity.

Raid 28th October 1940

Award of the George Medal to 2nd Lieutenant Ralph Henry Lee Royal Engineers, 9th Bomb Deposal Company, and Reginald Ernest Cooke, Platoon Commander F7 (Austin Aero Engine Co.Ltd) Home Guard.

London Gazette 11th/3rd/1941

Ralph Henry Lee:

A 550lb bomb with a delay action fuse fell in the machine shop of a factory employed on vital aircraft production work. After forty-five hours work it was exposed and the fuse found to be still ticking. Owing to the time, which had elapsed, explosion was probable at any moment. Lieutenant Lee cleared his men away and himself made a determined effort to remove the fuse, but after fifteen minutes work found he could not do so. He then got a crowbar and managed to extract the electrical part but the essential clockwork part, still ticking remained immovable with the detonators. Lee decided to fill the fuse pocket with water with a view to making the clock stop and subsequently filled the hole too, so as to provide a greater water pressure.

This was successful and the bomb was removed next morning. Lieutenant Lee was for thirty-five minutes working alone in what he well knew was most imminent danger.

Reginald Ernest Cooke[1]:

On 28th October 1940, a 55lb bomb containing a delay action fuse was located at factory and the clock was found to be still ticking. The bomb had been down for approximately forty-five hours and an explosion, from experience, was considered so imminent as to justify withdrawal of the working party. An attempt to remove the fuse failed and the officers concerned, together with Cook, was present the whole time, and withdrew to consider the matter.

In view of the importance of the factory it was decided to attack the fuse a second time using a heavy crowbar. Three persons were necessary but on removal of the ticking clock the detonators still remained intact. It was then decided to flood the pit in an endeavour to stop the clock and Cooke's assistance again proved invaluable in what turned out to be a successful operation, the bomb being successfully removed.

---

[1] *Cooke was the only Birmingham Home Guard Officer to receive the George Medal for bomb disposal.*

Raid 1st November 1940

Award of the George Medal to Alfred John Biggs, Captain, 9th Bomb Disposal Company, Royal Engineers.

London Gazette 22/1/194
At 1.30am on 1st November 1940 a 250-Kilogram bomb fell through the railway viaduct at Curzon Street. This was reported to No 9 Bomb Disposal Company at 1.45 am. Captain Biggs immediately set off with a sergeant to investigate the position. The bomb was found partially buried beneath the viaduct and in such a position that its explosion would seriously dislocate traffic for a considerable period. Captain Biggs immediately got to work and uncovered the fuse, which was still ticking and attempted to take it out, but the locking ring had jammed. By means of a hammer and chisel, the filling cap was taken off, the T.N.T washed out with a hosepipe and, with a crowbar, he levered out the fuse pocket. The work was completed at 2.30 am. The fuse exploded seven minutes after removal.

Though the circumstances attending and the fortunate outcome of this incident are somewhat striking, it is only one of many instances of equally courageous action by this officer who, by his conduct, inspires all ranks of the Company under his command.

Raid 1st to 2nd November 1940

Award of the George Medal to Robert Leslie Arnold, Foreman A.R.P Rescue Party.

London Gazette 21/3/1941
On November 1st at about 200 hours H.E. (High Explosive) destroyed Nos. 136, 8, 40 and 42 Guildford Street and four back to back houses at rear. Arnold undertook particularly hazardous personal work in carrying out the rescue of a Mr Astle who was got out alive by carefully burrowing through loose sliding debris.

He was located by driving a tunnel through the cellar of an adjoining house. He could not be got away from that side because of the weight of debris pinning him from the top. It was necessary, consequently, to tunnel through the debris from the outside. This was particularly dangerous because the debris being very loose, as surrounded by walls which were in danger of falling at any moment, and was partly on fire. Time was very limited and Arnold himself burrowed through until he reached Mr Astle, whom he then drew out through the hole so made. Arnold was well aware of the danger and that at any moment he might be overwhelmed by the collapse of his burrow because there was no time to place any timber in it.

Arnold has, since the beginning of raiding five months ago, been most conscientious and assiduous in his duties, he with his squad, having attended hundreds of incidents and rescued many persons, often in extremely dangerous circumstances. His squad, in fact, was the first one ever to be used in Birmingham.

Raid 12th to 13th November 1940

The award of the George Medal to Leonard George Potter, Chief Fire and A.R.P Officer, S. Smith & Sons (Motor Accessories) Ltd.

London Gazette 3rd/1st/1941

Potter, who is a Foreman in the factories, has devoted his spare time to acquiring knowledge of Fire Brigade and A.R.P work.

A Delayed Action bomb fell on the factory together with two High Explosive devices. Although he was told there was a chance of the bomb exploding at any moment, he called for volunteers and directed the pumping out of water from the hole in which the bomb was lodged and then for several hours he led his men in building a sandbag wall round the hole which was done for the purpose of reducing the effect of the explosion had the bomb gone off.

On another occasion he showed courage and devotion to duty in his handling of a fire caused by an oil bomb which, had he not directed the Fire Brigade efficiently, may have spread to a much larger section of the works and have more seriously held up production of urgent war supplies.

Location and date unknown

Award of the British Empire Medal to Mrs Amelia Matty, Head of works Night Canteen.

London Gazette 21st/2nd/1941

Mrs Matty was in charge of a Works Canteen when a heavy raid was in progress. She was the only woman that night on the factory site. Incendiaries had started several fires and there were a number of minor injuries. Mrs Matty proceeded, in a cool and efficient manner, to help in the first aid work. She was in the canteen when a high explosive bomb fell which caused considerable damage. A number of men were

Amelia Matty [1]

[1] *A photograph of Mrs Matty appeared in the Birmingham Gazette. 28/3/1941.*

injured and Mrs Matty, although herself badly shaken, immediately went to their assistance. Her cheerfulness and courage were in evidence throughout the night until the raid finished, and were important factors in maintaining morale.

Raids October, November and December 1940

The award of the (B.E.M) British Empire Medal to Henry Herbert Pickering, Group A.R.P Warden.

London Gazette 18th August 1941

During the many intensive air raids on the city during October, November and December 1940 Pickering's Group was the most heavily bombed group on the B. Division and extreme devastation was caused by paramine, high explosive and incendiary bombs including a great many of the explosive type.

During every one of these raids, Pickering could always be found where the danger was greatest, busily engaged putting out incendiary bombs, assisting those trapped and rendered homeless, utterly regardless of high explosive and incendiary bombs which were falling all around in an area which on many occasion, was literally floodlit by very large business premises which were on fire.

On Tuesday, 19th November 1940, two paramines fell in Grant Street on his group, demolishing about 80 houses, badly damaging about 200 others, and in which five persons were killed and twenty injured. Pickering saw these falling and being firstly under the impression that they were parachutists, ran towards them, and when only 100 yards away did he realise the true position, and threw himself flat on the ground. He fortunately escaped injury and immediately got up with the utmost coolness, caused the action report to be sent, then worked unceasingly through the night regardless of all danger, rendering assistance to trapped and homeless persons.

P.S.B.8. Wilfred Curnock, who was incident officer at Grant Street, speaks in

Group Warden H. H. Pickering [1]

---

[1] *A photograph and short article on Harry Pickering appeared in the, Birmingham Gazette 19/07/1941*

the highest terms of Pickering's devotion to duty, not only at the incident referred to, but on many occasions during air attacks.

As a result of enquiries, whilst appreciating there is probably no outstanding case of individual gallantry by Pickering, have no hesitation in saying that he has through the many air raids to which his group has been subjected, carried out his duties with utter disregard to the great danger to which he was undoubtedly exposed and worked so untiringly in his efforts to assist air raid victims that he has inspired such confidence in the whole of the wardens on his group, that they will follow him anywhere and do anything at his bidding.

This confidence has been reflected on many occasions.

Raid 19th November 1940

The award of the (B.E.M) British Empire Medal to ARP warden, Mrs Beatrice Withers[1].

London Gazette 14th February 1941.

During an air raid on Tuesday, November 19th Mrs Withers, an ARP Warden went to a post to request that an ambulance be sent to St Pauls road to take a woman to hospital.

After leaving the post, Mrs Withers returned to St Paul's Road to await the arrival of the ambulance, whilst standing on the pavement, an aerial torpedo dropped a few yards away and exploded; a flying fragment from the bomb struck her on the head, it tore a piece out of her steel helmet, cutting her over the left eye and rendered her unconscious. Immediately on recovering, however, she went to the house outside which she had been standing fighting her way through the debris, as the house had been very badly damaged by the explosion. With the assistance of Mr Poole, Senior Warden, she forced open the door and under very difficult conditions, got the sick women, her baby and four other children to the safety of the shelter.

Without resting for first aid attention, Mrs Withers went back to St Paul's Road and assisted in the rescue of other people who were

Mrs. Withers

[1] *There are pictures of Mrs Withers in the, Birmingham Gazette for 15/2/1941 and 11/3/1941. Both show the helmet, which she wore that night, and the damage to it is clear to see.*

trapped in their house. During the whole of this time, enemy planes were overhead and bombs were falling all round. Considerable damage was done to property and nine people were killed and many others seriously injured in the vicinity.

In carrying out her duties amidst this intense enemy activity and despite her own injury, it is felt that Mrs Withers displayed a high standard of courage and devotion to duty.

From The Evening Mail

Air raid Warden Mrs Beatrice Withers, a cheerful soul in her fifties, was worried about a young woman in St Paul's Road, Balsall Heath who had recently had a baby.

She told friends she was afraid the young woman might be developing blood poisoning, and while the "screamers" were coming down she tried to keep an eye on the house.

The screamers were high explosive bombs with a whistle attached to the fins. They were designed to add just another element of terror to air attacks.

It was about nine o'clock when Mrs. Withers saw 13-year -old Dennis Sharp watching the gunfire and the glow from the city outside his home at 21 St Paul's Road. "Go in the house," she said, "You 'll be safer down in the cellar."

His father Mr Alfred Sharp, his stepmother Edith Sharp and their seven children were all sheltering in the house that night. Many times they had spent nights in public shelters, but this night they stayed in the cellar.

Mrs Sharp had a cold and only that day there had been a public health message that people with heavy colds and other infections should not go into public shelters. Several members of the sharp family were not home. Eleven year-old May was still staying at Princess Alice Orphanage, Sutton Coldfield because there wasn't room for her in St Paul's Road.

Her Sister Jessie, who was 18, had been at the Princess Alice with her but was now back home with the family. Other brothers and sisters were serving in the Forces.

Some of the houses on St Paul's road were empty that night. Folk had gone to stay with friends or relations in other parts of the city. At number 24 Miss Edith Abel, a 30-year-old member of the staff of the Britannic Assurance Company and her sister Laura was having a cup of tea on their cellar steps. Ruefully they reflected that their Anderson shelter had been bone dry until the end of October. Now that all hell was let loose outside, it was full of water and useless.

The sudden explosion came just after nine o'clock. Mrs Withers was knocked to the ground and the two sisters were swept into the cellar of No 24 as the steps disintegrated beneath them. Mrs Withers bleeding from the head where a piece of shrapnel had pierced her helmet, scrambled up, blew her whistle and shouted for help.

A bomb that landed in the Sharp's back garden had wrecked 10 houses in the

Victorian Terrace. Police Constable Derek Taylor, a young man who knew the Able sisters, helped them out of their shattered house and took them to a public shelter. Mrs Withers with rescue workers and policemen began the search of the wreckage. Behind the battered door of one house the found the woman with a baby in her arms. "Save, my baby" she said, "never mind about me". Both were unharmed, but at the Sharp home at No 21 was a ghastly ruin.

Rescue workers had to hack their way through splintered woodwork, lumps of masonry and pull away the bricks on by one. During the hours that followed the bodies of seven members of the family were recovered, including Jessie and Dennis. Mrs Sharp was found very seriously injured and taken to hospital with little hope of recovery. Then after several hours work the rescuers heard a whimper. Beneath the body of Mrs Sharp they found the four-year-old girl Marjorie, conscious and unhurt.

Raid 19th November 1940

The award of the King's Commendation (K.C) to Police Constable A.238 John Ernest Franklin.

London Gazette 25th April 1941
Commendation given for actions when a parachute mine fell in Ashley Street during an air raid. (Ashley St was off Bristol Street near Bristol Street Motors).

Raid 19th November 1940

The award of the George Medal (G.M) to District Officer, Birmingham Fire Brigade, Calypso Clarence Gammon, and the King's Commendation (K.C) to Leading Fireman, James Hogan and Acting Officer, John Evans.

London Gazette 21st March 1941
On the night of the 19th November, District Officer Gammon was in charge, between 21.00 and 24.00 hours, of a fire at premises occupied by Messrs Partridge and Lawrence Ltd, No 45, Tenby Street North.

The premises were severely bombed by high explosive and incendiary bombs and were ablaze from end to end. They are completely enclosed by buildings and the only method to attack was through two covered passageways on either side of the factory.

Auxiliary Firemen Wilson, no. 1089, whilst engaged on the fire, ventured too far along one of the passage-ways at the side of the building, when the heat caused on wall of the building to collapse outwards and he was struck, rendered unconscious and buried by the debris.

Leading fireman Hogan, under whose direction Wilson was acting, heard the fall of debris and when he arrived on the scene all that he could see was a length of partially buried hose. He immediately went for assistance and District Officer Gammon went back with him.

He was able to locate Wilson and found that he was in a sitting position and surrounded by burning debris, with his legs pinned under a large concrete girder. The flames from the burning building were rapidly sweeping towards him.

With the aid of Acting Officer Evans and Leading Fireman Hogan, District Officer Gammon set about removing, with his hands, the red hot brickwork, and despite the fact that other portions of he wall were continually falling in, succeeded in reaching Wilson.

By this time the fire had almost reached him, but despite the intense heat and great risk which he knew he was running, District Officer Gammon succeeded in lifting the concrete girder from the trapped man's legs and extracted him.

Wilson was conveyed to Hospital when it was found that he had a broken Collar bone, a lacerated wound to the scalp and severe bruises. He has now made a complete recovery.

The three Officers concerned in the rescue all say that had not district Officer Gammon been able to free Wilson immediately they would have had to leave him as the heat was so intense and walls were continually falling. These Officers and particularly District Officer Gammon, who directed the rescue, displayed great courage and disregard for their own safety.

District Officer Gammon received burns to the neck and hands but continued to direct fire operations after the rescue without stopping to receive treatment.

During the time the rescue was being effected, the surrounding district was submitted to intense bombardment, including the dropping of land mines, and the whole of the area was reduced to ruins.

From The Orders and Medals Research Society: Spring 1987 Pages 35-39[1]

In an article by Marcel Nuijitens, owner of Officer Gammon's medals (with the exception of the G.M) the following additional information is given. Gammon, universally known as "Clip" was born in Whitstable in Kent and came from a seafaring family, hence his unusual name; which was that of a popular windjammer of the time. He was commended in 1911 and 1913 for his work with the fire Brigade. In the Great War he served in the Engineers and received the 1914-15 star, the Service Medal and Victory Medal.

---

[1] *In this article there is also pictures of Gammon and full discussion of all his awards.*

Raid November 1940

King's Commendation: Leslie Raymond Phillips, Clerical Assistant, Queens Hospital.

London Gazette 7th/2nd/1941
Leslie R Phillips, a bacteriological technician at the Queen's Hospital is commended for plucky work on the roof of the hospital, in November 1940.

He was extinguishing incendiary bombs in Bath Row when he saw another bomb fall on to the roof of the medical block of the hospital. Shouting to another man that he knew the way on to the roof, Phillips ran through the building, on to a flat roof, up a ladder laid on the slates, and covered the blazing bomb with sand. It had fallen through among the rafters and dealing with it was no easy task. He was not content to deal with bombs. While he was perched on the roof he also saved another man from death or serious injury. The man who had followed him on to the roof was under the impression that iron railings surrounded the whole of the roof, and began to slide down the slates. Phillips, however, knew that part of the roof was not protected, and just managed to grab the clothes of the other man as he began to slide.

Raid 19th – 20th November 1940
BSA Works Small Heath[1]

The award of:
George Medal: Albert William Bailey, Volunteer, 6th Birmingham Battalion, Home Guard; John Hadley, ARP Rescue Party; Alfred Frank Stevens, Works Electrician BSA Guns Ltd.

British Empire Medal: Arthur Richard Edmund Harris, Works Pipe Fitter BSA Guns Ltd; Alfred Walter Goodwin, Works Electrician, BSA Guns Ltd; John Hastings Beattie, Sub Section Leader; Joseph Topham, Section Leader; William Saragine, Volunteer, 6th Birmingham Battalion, Home Guard.

King's Commendation: Samuel Simpton Ashburner, Works Fitter; Edwyn Hoof, Works Electrician; Ernest Williams, Works Browner; All BSA Guns Ltd.

New Years Honours 9th January 1946
Member of the British Empire (Civil) Miss Ada Mary Deeming, Matron BSA Co Ltd.
British Empire Medal (Civil) Albert Slim, Grinder BSA Co Ltd.

---

[1] *There is a painting depicting the bombed factory in the*
Birmingham Museum and Art Gallery, by Charles Cundall.

Extracts From the London Gazette.

Albert William Bailey GM[1]
Alfred Frank Stevens GM

On the night of 19th-20th November 1940, Bailey was due to report at the BSA Home Guard for duty. Hearing bombing he arrived at Armoury Road, corner of the company's premises at 7 p.m. He remained on duty there helping them deal with incendiary bombs. He went to the Head quarters of the Home Guard at abut 9pm, here he met an officer who called for Home Guard volunteers to rescue those trapped in the debris of the "New Buildings", which had suffered a direct hit from enemy aircraft.

He first helped to rescue a member of the Home guard on the canal side of Heavy Auto and later with another Home Guard, got out two workmen from the same place.

He went to the other side of the debris, where he first helped a man out and then assisted a girl to escape. He tried to get through a hole lower down, but could not, so he returned to the first hole and crawled through but came to a large slab of concrete. From the other side he heard voices, he was able to knock a small hole through the concrete, through which he was able to thrust his torch; four men and a girl were huddled on the other side. He began to enlarge the hole but a steel girder stopped progress. He asked for assistance and was soon back in the hole with Alfred Stevens, an electrician, and an Oxy-acetylene apparatus. The fire above was burning fiercely and the heat was so intense that their clothes began to scorch. As they set to work other members of the rescue party crawled along the hole bringing with them a hose, which they kept playing on them. It was a slow job and at one time Bailey had to stand with his hands above his head supporting a piece of masonry, which threatened to fall and trap them. Eventually a way was cleared and the girl was rescued first, but the hole was too narrow for the men, and again the process of cutting steel away started again. The two rescuers were being scalded as water from the hoses being played on the fire above trickled through the hot debris, but the hole was enlarged and the four men were brought out, one at a time. The rescuers were saturated with oil and water and Bailey finally collapsed near the entrance and was taken home in an ambulance. For Stevens, another ordeal was to come.

---

[1] *Article on William Bailey in the Birmingham Gazette, Wednesday, 12 Feb, 1941, page 5.*

John Hadley GM
Alfred Frank Stevens GM
Arthur Richard Edmund Harris BEM
Alfred Walter Goodwin BEM
Joseph Topham BEM
Edwyn Hoof KC

When the four storey heavy industrial, reinforced concrete, building collapsed, a man and a girl had taken shelter under a bench on the ground floor where they were buried under the wreckage. Other members of the rescue parties declined to act as they considered the case hopeless. Knowing the risk, the above volunteered for a further rescue attempt. As the hole was enlarged the men went in, forming a human conveyer to pass back the pieces of metal and masonry as they prised free or cut away to pass back the pieces of metal and masonry. After three hours of effort and three cylinders of Oxy-acetylene had been used, they could see the trapped victims. The man and girl lying pinned under the heavy wooden bench, eventually Stevens was able to get close enough to saw the bench into two but it could not be moved due to the weight of girders and wreckage resting on it. Eventually a rope was fastened to part of the bench and was pulled clear first the girl and then the man were rescued.

The precarious nature of the weight of debris, together with an adjacent building, made any form of propping or support for a tunnel impossible. The building was burning all the time and work was suspended several times so that water could be directed in to the tunnel. It was seemed certain that if left the couple would have either burned to death or drowned. Most of the work was done in a prone position, Stevens at times was working upside down with men holding his ankles. With no protection from the Oxy-acetylene burner which was spluttering due to fire fighting water. Several times enemy planes circled low and the advice of "Take Cover!" was ignored.

When it is remembered that the building was completely demolished and the debris was sitting under its own weight and the effects of fire, there can be no doubt of the heroism and self -sacrifice displayed by the rescuers who were throughout in the foremost peril of their lives.

Before helping Hadley and Stevens, Topham and two other Home Guards rescued four members of the Home Guard who were trapped under the debris of an air raid shelter which had been hit. Topham had also been to and assisted in the rescue of the five people trapped in Number One Rescue Hole.

John Beattie BEM
Several rescues from the middle block were effected by Beattie, who had just returned to the New Building, when it was hit. As the bomb exploded the workers dived for cover under the machines. Beattie found himself under a bench where

the blast had blown him and went to one of the wrecked workshops. He found the entrance blocked by debris, but there was a hole through, which he managed to force his way. By the light of his torch he could see arms and legs protruding from the overturned machinery, some were dead. He climbed over the wreckage and found a woman. He took her to the hole, through which she was assisted by other rescue workers. Four times Beattie went back, each time bringing an injured worker out with him. He held up lumps of concrete to prevent them from falling into the hole, and he was saturated with oil and water. On the fifth journey he found fire had broken out and the flames had taken a hold. He tried to go back a sixth time but found it was impossible, the shop was a blazing mass. At the end of some hours he was completely exhausted and was evacuated by the medical authorities.

Samuel S. Ashburner KC
Ernest Williams KC
Throughout the night rescue parties ceaselessly probed the wreckage. Hours after the bombs had fallen; Samuel Ashburner saw a woman's foot moving under a machine. With assistance of another man the machine was raised sufficiently for her to be pulled free. Several rescues were also effected by Ernest Williams.

Frank Knight KC
He was conspicuous in his endeavours to rescue the wounded and worked continuously for several hours, until exhausted. Being of small stature he crawled into various holes under the debris on several occasions to locate the position of people trapped there. He was to a very great extent successful in their efforts and it was partly on the information he gave that successful evacuation of several people took place.

George J. Treen KC
George Wilson KC
For devotion to duty. Both these men made several trips from the casualty centre to fetch blankets and comfort for the injured from the guardroom. The anti-aircraft barrage was very severe at the time and bombs were falling, but these men showed intense willingness to serve although neither was in possession of a steel helmet. These men are very young and it is all the more to their credit that they showed absolutely no fear during the whole of this very severe bombardment.

William Saragine BEM[1]
At an early stage in the raid the external telephone system was put out of action. Additional fire fighting units were needed so Saragine volunteered and on a motor cycle he called at the fire stations in the area. The anti-aircraft barrage was severe and high explosive and incendiaries were dropped continuously. Three times he was

---

[1] *Birmingham Gazette, 8th April 1941, there is a photo of William Saragine as well as an article about why he did not wear his medal - he had been given the wrong ribbon and he did not want to offend any one.*

blown from his machine by bomb blasts and on at least one occasion he passed within a few feet of a delayed action bomb. Saragine took his life in his hands during the whole period he was on duty.

Raid 19th to 20th November 1940

British Empire Medal: Edward Lamb, General Labourer

London Gazette 24/4/1941
A high explosive bomb demolished dwelling – in Hope Street – Lamb ran to the scene, followed by others, and commenced to remove the debris. One person was rescued but two others were still trapped. One of these, a women, had her legs fixed close to a grate in which a fire was burning. Rescue work was very hazardous as surrounding houses were almost collapsing. More debris had to be removed, and Lamb worked in the cavity he had made for three hours.

As a result of the courageous action and perseverance of Lamb three persons were rescued alive.[1]

From a report to Steel House Lane Police Station 26th Dec 1940
The two remaining persons were sitting in chairs, facing a fire, with the roof across the top of them, and one was pinned against the fire grate which had a fire in it. It was an elderly woman, she shrieked with pain, and I could see her legs were forced against the hot bars of the grate. Water was brought and I poured jugs full on to the grate and the burning coals to put out the fire, cool the grate and relieve the woman in contact with it. We were able to cool it down a good bit in this way. A H.E bomb fell and demolished a number of other houses about 20 yards away, some went to cover but a few remained with me. I could see the woman pinned against the grate would have to be moved before we could get to the third person who was also facing towards the fire. I got a heavy hammer with me, and I smashed some of the grate with it. It was at this point that a police man with two stripes came with a special constable, and the Acting Sergeant said "come on chum, you have a rest, I think you have done well, let me have a go" I got out of the excavation I had made and he got in.

He poured more water on to the fire, and with my hammer smashed the grate, and was then able to pull out both persons, a man and woman. They were both injured and I think they were taken away to hospital.

Raid 19th to 20th November 1940

British Empire Medal: John Herbert Christie, Police Sergeant; Robert Edward Grills, War Reserve Constable; John Clark, Property Repairer.

---

[1] *Birmingham Gazette, 12th February 1941, Short description of his act of heroism and the fact that he lived on Mole St, Sparkbrook.*

London Gazette 4/4/1941

A H.E bomb demolished a dwelling house, – 89 & 80 Murdock Road Handsworth and 5 Union Road Handsworth- trapping the occupants.

Christie and Grills worked through the wreckage by removing bricks with their hands. After one woman had been released it was found that a supporting a wall was about to collapse. Clark propped this up with timber, part of it fell, and he was injured by falling debris. The three men then continued their work and succeeded in releasing another woman.

The rescue work was done in extremely difficult and dangerous conditions. In addition to the amount of debris overhead, with the possibility of collapse of parts of the house, water was pouring from broken pipes and gas was escaping.

During the whole time the area was subjected to a heavy bombardment of high explosive and incendiary bombs

Christie, Grills and Clark acted in the most courageous manner at very grave risk to their lives.

Christie (Centre) and Grills (Right)

From a Report to Recommendation Committee.

After some time they continued to call out and then got a reply from the voice of a woman. After removing still further brickwork and timber, they came across one of the occupants a Miss Chambers They got her out, suffering from a badly cut face, and quite near to her was another woman named Mrs Strickley, whom they also rescued and after First Aid treatment, they were removed to Dudley Road Hospital. Both these Officers continued to search for the third woman and after a little while got to her head but she was pinned down so badly that it was impossible for them to get her free. At this time she was alive and they spoke to her and attempted to comfort her all they could. Still no Rescue Squad arrived. They continued at great risk still further attempts to get this woman out, but failed and they then found that she had died. This woman, whose name was Miss Davie was removed later by the Rescue Squad. The first two women, so far as I can ascertain, are still living.

Raid 19th to 20th November 1940

George Medal: Andrew Sanders, 2074517 Corporal (Acting Lance Sergeant) Royal Engineers.

London Gazette 2/2/1941

Andrew Sanders has been engaged in bomb disposal since August 1940. He has taken charge on at least five Category 'A' excavations involving work on bombs at short intervals after falling. He has twice been injured during operations but this had no effect on his knees and capacity for taking on any job.

19th November 1940

A 250 kilogram bomb fell alongside some condensers at Nechells Gas Works at 11.30 pm. The report was not received at company Headquarters until 6.30am on the 20th. He volunteered to take charge of the working party and by his energy and steadiness kept the party working until the bomb was finally disposed of at 12.30pm.

2nd February 1941

A bomb was lodged beneath the foundations of a house in Dolobran Road, Sparkbrook. The ground was found to be extra bad and consequently underpinning was necessary. At a depth of fourteen feet, during excavation, water burst through a cast iron main causing timbers to give way. One man was pinned in the hole and the underpinning commenced to fall away. He ordered his party away, with the exception of one man, secured himself by rope and descended to the trapped man. He managed to extricate the man and brought him to the surface. His prompt act saved the mans life, as the wall collapsed into the hole.

Sgt. Sanders

From: Birmingham Evening Mail 2/3/1984

George (Sandy) Saunders had been in the TA Royal Engineers in 1939, he was discharged from the Army in July 1942, suffering from gastric ulcers. He moved from Birmingham to Redditch where he died in 1962, at the age of 42.

Raids 19th and 20th November 1940

George Medal: John Henry Rouson, Temporary Sub-Lieutenant, Royal Naval Volunteer Reserve; and Wilson Boyce, Seaman Royal Navy, P/JX 198295

London Gazette 23/1/1941

19th November 1940

When Sub-Lieutenant W.H Taylor arrived at Burberry Street and Gerrard Street, Birmingham, Rouson was having great difficulty with a parachute mine, the clock of the fuse had already ticked once and the locking ring would not start. They tried together but they bent the spanner and dislocated Rouson's thumb. They reset the thumb and tried to drill the locking ring out but pressure leaked out of the horn. One of them tried to hold the horn squeezed while the other drilled. They decided that the mine was due to explode any minute and that further work on the fuse would lead to suicide. An attempt was made to burn the mine with Thermite but it exploded and damaged many houses.

20th November 1940

At 11 Reginald Street, Saltley, a mine was standing vertically and partly buried about three steps up the staircase of the tenement building. In complete darkness, one worked and the other held the torch it was not possible to start the locking ring and the fuse started ticking. They ran for their lives and when they were thirty feet away the mine exploded and damaged thirty to forty houses. Both were wounded and taken to hospital. It is incredible that they are still alive.

Rouson has rendered safe nine mines, burned out two and countermined one. Wilson Boyce, this man has assisted his officer in a most gallant and able manner. He was shocked by the explosion of the last mine as he was forced to go much closer than usual to chase away civilians who were too curious.

From a Birmingham Newspaper
(Story deals with a series of incidents of bomb disposal)

Next day, November 20th Taylor[1] and Rouson were summoned to a house in Reginald Road, Saltley. The usual pillar-box bomb was there wedged in the buildings but at least the bomb fuse was accessible. Something had gone wrong with the safety mechanism on the fuse. The official report said, "The clock started and only ran for ten seconds before the mine exploded".

---

[1] *Rouson was assisted in Birmingham with his work on mine disposal by Lieutenant W.H. Taylor RNVR, who was awarded the George Cross for his work at Uxbridge.*

Raid 22nd/23rd November 1940

King's Commendation: Leslie Hartland, Volunteer, Francis James Peacock, Volunteer, Post Office Home Guard Unit: Later part of 27th (Birmingham) Warwickshire Battalion.

London Gazette 27/5/1941

On the night of 22nd / 23rd November 1940 during an intense enemy air attack on Birmingham the guard room of the GPO Home Guard battalion at the Post Office depot received a direct hit from a high explosive bomb. One of the guards was killed outright and another had his leg blown off.

Two other members of the guard, volunteers Hartland and Peacock, rendered first aid to the injured man and left him in charge of the first aid party. They then went in search of a doctor. At this time the bombing was intensive and the streets were being machine-gunned. They found a doctor at a shelter about a quarter of a mile from the depot and Peacock guided him to the First Aid Post while Hartland went to the nearest First Aid Station about half a mile away to bring an ambulance.

Raid 22nd / 23rd November 1940

British Empire Medal: Walter Heath[1], Works Fireman, and Home Guard Volunteer.

London Gazette 28/2/1941

On the night of 22nd November 1940 the works firemen on duty were Walter Heath, Captain of the works Fire Brigade and Fireman W Green. During the raid incendiary bombs fell onto the works, Heath and Green tackled and extinguished a number of these but one pierced the roof of a small storeroom on the top floor. A hose was run up a winding staircase in the dark and it was an hour before the fire was under control.

An oil bomb fell and exploded, setting fire to a pile of timber in an adjoining yard, which then spread to the works Heath and Green were protecting. The 120-gallon pump was brought into action and two jets were directed from opposite sides of the blaze by the two firemen. But this procedure was founded to be inadequate; a jet was needed to be directed down on to the fire and on to the roofs of the single-storied outbuildings to prevent a conflagration. Accordingly, Heath ascended to the flat roof, and with his hose running up the side of the wall he stood for over seven hours unceasingly fighting the flames, which, through his effort never succeeded in spreading to the vital workshops High explosives fell continually, one falling on the spot in the yard where Heath had been previously standing. For the first hour of his ordeal he was alone, as assistance could not

---

[1] *There is a photo of Walter Heath receiving his B.E.M outside Buckingham Palace in 4th Battalion Royal Warwickshire Regiment. (Birmingham Home Guard). 1948 private publication.*

immediately be spared. In all, Heath put in fifteen hours continual duty, refusing to rest until all danger passed.

The works are situated in a high target area alongside the Grand Union Canal and near where the Birmingham to London railway cross's the Birmingham to Coventry road, and near other road junctions.

Raid 22nd / 23rd November 1940

George Medal: Rueben Haigh, Platoon Commander, 9th Birmingham Battalion Home Guard; Albert Edward Smith and John Thomas Bonning Gasholder Repairmen, City of Birmingham Gas Department.
King's Commendation: Sidney Alexander Tyler, Volunteer, 9th Birmingham Battalion Home Guard, Alfred Bowles, and G.T. Phillips Assistant Valvemen, City of Birmingham Gas Department.[1]

London Gazette 31/1/1941
At about 8pm on 22nd November 1940 a number of incendiary bombs fell on the Wagon Repair Shops site and on the gas works (at Saltley). Haigh was P.19 Company Home Guard, Duty Officer and after one or two small fires in P19 Company Home Guard area had received attention, with S.A Tyler he proceeded to the Gas Works. They found two fires in the coal stack and extinguished them. Two "smoke screen" containers had been ignited and were burning with considerable flame. These, in the absence of equipment for dealing with oil fires were extinguished with some difficulty. There was a plume of flame in the crown of one Gasholder; at the time the crown of the gasholder was some 200 feet high. Haigh, taking the initiative and with three other men, S.A Tyler, A Bowles and G.T. Phillips, ascended to the crown of the holder carrying sacks and after considerable effort extinguished the fire and partially stopped the escape of gas with bags and clay.

Lieut. R. Haigh   Mr A. E. Smith   Mr J. T. Bonning   Lieut S.A. Tyler

[1] *In a chapter of 'Birmingham in the Second World War', there are photos of Haigh, Bonning and Smith as well as photos of the damage to the gas works.*

Another aperture in the crown of the holder through which gas was escaping but not burning was dealt with in the same way. No protective equipment was carried. The raid was still in progress with bombs dropping in the vicinity and the flames from the holder must have provided continuous beacon. The action taken by Haigh and the other three men not only promptly removed the beacon, but also saved a considerable quantity of gas from escaping.

London Gazette 31/1/1941
An incendiary bomb struck the crown of a gasholder in Saltley Gas Works at an acute angle, causing a long split and then emerged through the side of the holder. A.E. Smith and J.T. Bonning with assistance attempted to extinguish the flame with clay; they were, however, unsuccessful. Later, together with several Auxiliary Fire Service men climbed the holder again and used more clay in trying to get the fire out, but still without result. It was then decided that as all the clay heaped over the hole had dried out with the heat and had to be removed before a further attempt could be made with fresh supplies of wet clay; this was successful. At the time, anti-aircraft fire was heavy and bombs could be heard dropping fairly close to the works, but the men carried on at great risk to themselves and the flames were extinguished.

Raids on the 23rd November and 11th December 1940

George Cross: William R. Mosedale, Station Officer and Rescue Officer Birmingham Fire Brigade.
King's Commendation: Mrs Mary Barrow M.D; Alfred White, Fireman: Charles Albert Wilford, Fireman: George William Metcalfe, Fireman.

London Gazette 28/3/1941[1]
Incident one
At 02.51 hours on the night of the 23rd November, Station Officer Mosedale was ordered to proceed with breathing apparatus to 110, Yardley Wood Road, where three people had been trapped in the dwelling house.

Whilst the rescue van was proceeding along Showell Green Lane, a high explosive bomb burst 20 yards in front of it, causing a crater 30 feet wide and 20 feet deep. Despite the fact that the machine was pulled up as quickly as possible, on coming to a standstill two thirds of its length was in the crater, causing damage to the under carriage and sump.

Although considerably shaken by the blast, Station Officer Mosedale went on foot to a near-by Fire Station in Court Road, Sparkhill, and then got in touch with an adjoining A.R.P Depot. The Officer in charge put at his disposal a car and driver,

---
[1] *There is a photo of Station Officer Mosedale in the 'Birmingham Gazette' 29/3/1941, as well as an account of the rescues.*

W. R. Mosedale and a close up of his George Cross Medal.

and with two sets of breathing apparatus and the Novita Reviving Appliance which he took from the rescue van, Station Officer Mosedale went on to Yardley Wood Road.

On arrival, he found that a dwelling house that been struck by a high explosive bomb and demolished, and although three persons had been rescued, one was still buried under the debris on the ground floor at the rear of the house.

Station Officer Mosedale, with the assistance of an A.R.P Rescue Squad, succeeded, despite an intense bombardment, in getting to the man and removing sufficient debris from him to enable him to sit up. He was then given oxygen and was able to free himself a little so that he could be extricated. He was then removed to Selly Oak Hospital and is progressing satisfactorily.[1]

Incident two

At 22.30 hours on the 11th December, it was reported that an Auxiliary Fire Station (Stating 5/4 Grantham Road, Sparkbrook) had been completely demolished by a high explosive bomb of the largest type.

Station Officer Mosedale was immediately sent with the rescue van and was accompanied by fireman G Metcalfe, A.R White and C Wilford. The squad arrived at Grantham Road at 22.40 hours and were told by a Warden and the police that a number of Auxiliary Firemen were trapped in the Station and civilians in an adjoining house which had also been demolished.

---

[1] *There is a longer version of this incident and an interview with Station Officer Mosedale in a work on recipients of the George Cross published in the early 1960s*

Station Officer Mosedale ascertained as quickly as he could the position of the Control Room in which it was known that certain men were on duty when the Station was hit. He then commenced tunnelling and propping operations. Hundreds of tons of debris covered the site and tunnelling was undertaken in very hazardous circumstances. Station Officer Mosedale, by reason of his training and the fact that he had worked in a Coal Mine before joining the fire Brigade, realised the danger which he was facing.

In order to reach the Control Room he decided to tunnel. When the first tunnel was completed and the control Room reached, he found that there were still men whom he could not extricate and he then carried our another tunnelling operation from another direction and again entered the Control Room. Ultimately five men were found, one of whom was dead and the other four injured.

Station Officer Mosedale crawled through the tunnel which had been made and administered oxygen to the men who were in a very low condition. The oxygen revived them , however, and it was then possible for them to be got out through the tunnel.

Station officer Mosedale then made a further survey of the building to see if it was possible to make an entrance to two cellars, in one of which civilians were trapped and in the other auxiliary Firemen. The entrance to the cellar of the private house was found to be full of debris and Station Officer Mosedale directed operations for removing this, only to find that the cellar itself had collapsed. He nevertheless persevered, and after a time found that seven people were trapped, three of whom had been killed outright when the roof collapsed. He gave oxygen to the

Three Birmingham firemen—G. W. Metcalfe, C. A. Wilford and A. White (left to right), all of the Central Station, who were commended in last night's " London Gazette," for the rescue work when an A.F.S. Station and adjoining boarding house was wrecked in a raid.   Dr. Mary Ellen Barrow, of Birmingham, who crawled into the wreckage to administer morphia to the trapped victims, is also commended for her courage.

remaining four and succeeded in freeing them from debris and extricating them. He had, in the meanwhile sent for ambulances and first aid squads and the injured were removed to Hospital.

To reach the Firemen it was again necessary to tunnel, and Station Officer Mosedale immediately commenced their work. The hazards to be faced were similar to those, which he had found in entering the Control Room, but he nevertheless completed the tunnel and entered the cellar. There were six men in the cellar, four were alive and two dead. The men who were alive were given oxygen, and despite their injuries, were safely removed. He then fastened a lifeline to the dead men and they were withdrawn through the tunnel.

The propping of the tunnel through such difficult material had necessarily been a hazardous operation, and whilst a second fireman was being removed, the tunnel collapsed completely.

These operations were carried out continuously from 22.40 hours on the 11th December until 12.20 hours on the 12th December and during the early hours under a most intense bombardment. Throughout them Station Officer Mosedale displayed resources an initiative, coupled with complete disregard for his personal safety.

Dr. Mary Barrow, of 184 Stratford Road, attended throughout the operations for the rescue of men at the Grantham Road Station. She displayed the greatest courage and resource and frequently entered the tunnel, which had been made to administer morphia to the injured persons. Station Officer Mosedale, and the regular Firemen in his squad, have reported that many of the persons trapped would undoubtedly have died but for Dr Barrow's gallantry. During the whole of the operation she showed a complete disregard for her personal safety.

Eleven persons were rescued alive and seven bodies were subsequently recovered.[1]

Letters Sent to Station Officer Mosedale.
142 Wright St
Small Heath
Birmingham 10

Dear Mr Mosedale
Will you please except enclosed as a gift of personal thanks for your kindness shown to me on the night of December 11th 1940, for which I shall never forget. I think you were simply fine and worked so hard for the release to safety of us all.

Yours sincerely
J Allwood (Miss)
(from No3 Grantham Road)

---

[1] *Station Officer Mosedale was born in 1894, in Hope St. In 1908 he enlisted in the Territorial Battalion of the Royal Warwickshire Regiment, and in 1910 he joined the 50th. Royal Lancers.*

66 Birchwood Cres
Sparkbrook
Birmingham 12
31/3/1941

Dear Sir

It was with surprise that it said in the local press on Saturday, that you had been awarded the George Cross and realised that it was you who gave me the oxygen when I was buried at 110 Yardley Wood Road, on the night of 22nd November last.

I had a comminuted fracture of the pelvis and a dropped foot; however, I am now out of hospital and back at work again, still wearing an iron, but otherwise perfectly well.

I fully realise that I probably owe my life to you and your persistence and courage in bringing the oxygen cylinder to me.

I take this opportunity of thanking you most sincerely, but inadequately for all that you did for me and other people at later dates.

Believe me I am, Yours most sincerely

Geoffrey T. Shepherd[1]

Raid 23rd November 1940

King's Commendation: Albert Edward Judd (Juddy) Birmingham Co-operative Society Milk Roundsman.

London Gazette 1/8/1941

On the night of 23rd November 1940, gave the fire alarm when a building was bombed, rescued a man and his son, treated wounded persons.

Judd, a volunteer of the Green Lane first Aid Post, Small Heath was on duty during an air raid, 23rd November, 1940 when he commandeered a bus and took a number of injured people to the East Birmingham Hospital. The raid was still in progress and bombs were falling around the area. He later went to Whitmore Road and rescued 15 horses from stables in danger of catching on fire. He took the horses to the relative safety of Small Heath Park.

Birmingham Evening Mail Interview[2]

It was during the November 1940 blitz that Juddy experienced his finest hour. He was on duty on the Coventry Road, Small Heath when he heard the sirens go and the raid start. He immediately thought of his beloved horses and rushed to the Whitmore Road Stables to see if they were alright.

"Then a policeman stopped me and asked me to take eight or nine injured people

---

[1] *Original letters in Mosedale's own scrap book in Birmingham City Museum.*
[2] *This article contains further background information on Albert Judd and a number of photographs of him.*

By the KING'S Order the name of
Albert Edwin Judd,
Milk Roundsman,
Birmingham
was published in the London Gazette on
1 August, 1941.
as commended for brave conduct in
Civil Defence.
I am charged to record His Majesty's
high appreciation of the service rendered.

Winston S. Churchill

Prime Minister and First Lord
of the Treasury

King's Commendation awarded to Edward Judd (Juddy)

to the nearest hospital. I commandeered a bus and hung on outside the cab shouting directions to the driver, because there were no lights and the bombs were still falling" said Juddy.

He managed to get the bus through to the East Birmingham Hospital, Green Lane. He then returned to Whitmore Road, where the stables had been hit. He managed to get all the horses into the safety of Small Heath Park.

Juddy was commended for his brave action by Lord Dudley and presented with his award at a dinner held at the Botanical Gardens.[1]

Raids 14th and 24th November 1940

British Empire Medal: Arthur Ellis Green, Driver 2014169 Royal Engineers, No 9 Bomb Disposal Company.

London Gazette 30/9/1941
This driver has been continuously engaged since September 1940 as Batman Driver to an officer. During this period it has been his duty to drive his officer on night and day reconnaissance, both in Birmingham and Coventry and he has been out during nearly every major raid in both these cities. He had accompanied this officer on over 200 reconnaissance, approximately 70 of which during the night.

Incident 'A' November 14th 1940 Coventry
Driver Green was called out with his officer to proceed to Coventry. They arrived

---

[1] *Albert Judd or 'Juddy' as he was universally known became a popular local celebrity in his later years, giving talks on local radio about his experiences as a milkman.*

there to find nearly all roads impassable and a heavy concentration of bombs falling on the City. Owing to his determination his officer was enabled to reach Central Control and immediately to set out for the Daimler Factory from which a call had been received. After this one reconnaissance further progress could only be made on foot and he accompanied his officer throughout the night. During the night one bomb fell approximately 50 yards away throwing him the ground; despite a severe shaking he carried on. He remained a duty with his officer continuously from 1930 hours on 14th November until 23.00 hours on 16th November, and his conduct throughout this period is beyond praise.

Incident 'B' November 24th 1940 Birmingham
A mine was being detonated on Highgate Common. Owing to a misunderstanding (not the Drivers fault) his officer, after lighting the safety fuse of the demolition charge, was left stranded approximately 80 yards from the mine in the only bit of cover available (a bank 3ft high). This Driver, who had driven his car into cover some 300 yards away, saw the Officer's position and without hesitation, turned his car and drove back over open ground. The Officer was able to jump on the running -board of the car and escaped an explosion, which followed in approximately one minute after being picked up.

Raids 27th November and 12th December 1940

British Empire Medal: Horace Elliott, 2036910 Lance-Sergeant Royal Engineers, 9 Bomb Disposal Company.

London Gazette 30/9/1941
Incident one
On the 27th November 1940 a 250 kilo bomb fell in the Singer Motor works, Small Heath, Birmingham and was placed in Category 'A'. This NCO was given charge of the working party which commenced operations two and a half hours after the bomb fell and whilst the raid was still in progress. Chiefly owing to his initiative and energy the bomb was uncovered within five hours and successfully removed.

Incident two
On the 12th December 1940, this sergeant, then a junior NCO, played a very prominent part in the work on the bomb which fell at the BSA Guns Ltd, Small Heath, Birmingham, at 1.30 am. He worked continuously with very brief intervals for rest from 3am, on the 12th December until 2pm, 14th December.
    Lance Sergeant Elliott had worked continuously on bombs since August 1940,

and has displayed great courage and initiative in his work. He was engaged on one bomb, which exploded, causing fatal casualties: although badly shaken himself he refused, owing to pressure of work at the time, to remain off duty.

Raid 4th December 1940

George Medal: Edward Knibbs, General Dealer, aged 55.

At about 7.20pm, on Wednesday 4th December 1940, a high explosive bomb fell in Great Russell Street, Hockley, demolishing houses number 7 and 8. Three persons were trapped in number 7, Emily Davis aged 20 and Marjorie Davis aged 16 and Arthur Knowles aged 17 years. Knibbs climbed over debris and rescued the younger girl. There was a small hole in the debris leading down to the kitchen fire, which was still burning and Knibbs being slightly built, went down the hole and with the aid of a torch, which was held for him, he saw the youth with his head under a beam. He released his head and dragged him out. He then saw a girl pinned under a beam in a chair and he had to saw the seat and one arm off the chair to release her. He rescued her after a considerable time. Mr Knibbs was working in a cramped position, close to the fire grate for eighty minutes and there was considerable risk of the house further collapsing and trapping him. Further bombs were also dropped in the vicinity during the time rescue work was being undertaken. Mr Knibbs sustained an injury to his right eye.

Dr Rosenthal, who was present, states he was very much impressed with the conduct of Mr Knibbs, he acted in a most courageous manner on the occasion, he worked and rescued these people without regard to his own safety and recommended that his action is worthy of some recognition.

Birmingham Evening Dispatch 25th June 1941, page 3.[1]

Raid hero scared, couldn't sleep for nights because he has to see King. Bombs don't trouble raid hero Mr Arthur Edward Knibbs, 109 Hampton Street, Hockley, but when he had to see the King to receive the George Medal for his bravery Mr Knibbs said, *'I've never been so scared I all my life, I could not sleep for nights before.*

I don't know why as the King is a most charming fellow. He shook my hand very firmly, asked me what I did and if business was good. He also expressed the wish that every thing would go well for me in the future.

I had a grand time and I spent several days seeing all the sights of London and having a good look round. I think I can say I am the happiest and proudest man in Birmingham at the moment'.

Mr Knibbs who was one of the first Birmingham men to receive the George Medal from the King was awarded it for his bravery when rescuing people from a bombed house during the blitz. He was on his way home from work at the time.

---

[1] *There is a photo of Mr Knibbs wearing his three 1914-18 war medals at the top of the original article.*

Raid 11th December 1940

George Medal: Walter Thomas Bates, Acting Deputy Superintendent ARP Casualty Service.
Thomas Simpson, Platoon Commander 6th Birmingham Battalion, Home Guard.

London Gazette 21/3/1941

During the air raid, which took place on the night of The 11th December, Kings Road ARP Depot received two direct hits by High Explosive devices. At the time forty-six personnel were in the clearing station and the first bomb dropped alongside; causing walls to collapse and the concrete roof to fall in.

Mr Bates immediately entered the building – which was in danger of collapse – in order to rescue injured personnel and render first aid to these who could not immediately be rescued. By his own efforts he rescued five injured persons who were trapped under a grinder and twelve others who were not injured. He then inspired the latter to assist him in rescuing the remainder of the personnel. In all, twenty-two of the forty-six personnel were injured (including one fatal and fourteen seriously) and the remainder were affected by shock.

Soon after he made his first rescue the second bomb fell, causing Mr Bates to be

The Decontamination Building, Kings Road, Tyseley after the raid on 11th Dec.

flung to the ground. Regardless of flying debris; the increased danger of collapse of the buildings and the possibility of the boilers in the cleansing station bursting, Mr Bates continued his rescue work. By his total disregard for his own safety Mr Bates won the respect and admiration of all concerned.

On the night of December 11th 1940, Platoon Commander, Thomas Simpson, actively assisted in he rescue of several persons who were trapped beneath debris when an ARP Depot was hit. He had to crawl through the debris while men supported the props and there was great danger of other parts of the building collapsing on him. He managed to saw through steel pipes and remove the debris which was lying across the trapped persons. He showed conspicuous gallantry and devotion to duty.

From a Letter in Mr Minton's Possession
Referring to your article in the Birmingham Evening Mail about the Birmingham Blitz November 1940, and the medal awarded to W Bates. I would like to inform you that the place in question was the Public Works Depot Kings Road, Tyesley, which was at that time an ARP ambulance and resource station and I was an ambulance Driver/Attendant. It was my Mother Mrs Gladys Gisbourne who was trapped under the grinder. Fortunately she was amongst the first to be rescued and removed to the casualty clearing station at Church Road School Yardley.

The citation for Mr Bates was in essence true, but factually inaccurate. The people who were reported to be sheltering were in fact on duty, awaiting further instructions. It was not a shelter but a purpose built structure, and was the cause of great dispute amongst the personnel.

Raid 11th December 1940

King's Commendation: John Henry Porthero, Assistant Clerk of Works, Public Works Department: Cyril Walter Tart, Police Constable A.77, Steelhouse Lane Police Station.

London Gazette 20/6/1942
On 11th December, assisted in the removal of parachute mine, which fell on a premises in Digbeth. (The premises concerned were Morgan's the pork butchers and sausage maker next door to Digbeth police Station)

They rendered very valuable assistance for four hours within 15 feet of an unexploded bomb. Which courageous conduct assisted the Naval Mine Disposal Officer to render the parachute mine harmless.

Raid 12th December 1940

George Medal: Gilbert Ernest Stubbs, Lieutenant Royal Naval Volunteer Reserve: Frederick Garmory, P/SSX 23907 Able Seaman Royal Navy.

London Gazette 27/6/1941

Lieutenant Stubbs had dealt with ten unexploded mines and has shown quite cool courage and common sense.

On 12th December 1940 a mine fell into the cellar of a house in Windsor Road, Birmingham. The hole was big enough to let in some light and it was possible to crawl out through a hole in case of need but there would have been poor prospect of escaping had the fuse started; with great coolness and common sense Stubbs, with the help of Able Seaman Garmory rendered it safe.

An instance of Stubbs work, was when a mine penetrated a roof of an outside lavatory in Old Nichol Street, Bethnal Green, London. Owing to the damage caused by its fall, the mine was completely jammed with a lot of rubble around it. The only means of access was by crawling through the hole in the roof and this meant that he had no possible chance of escape should the fuse start. Nothing daunted he rendered the mine safe successfully.

Able Seaman Garmory has also helped in the work of rendering mines safe for a long time and besides being very reliable has continuously displayed courage and coolness in the face of danger.

Raid 14th December 1940

George Medal: James Henry Hyndman Kessack, Lieutenant Royal Australian Naval Volunteer Reserve: John McFetridge, Seaman Royal Naval Reserve.

London Gazette 27/6/1941

James H H Kessack, has now dealt with ten unexploded mines and showed persistent courage and resolution.

The first mine that he dealt with was at Birmingham on 14th December 1940. This had fallen into a clubroom, was covered with debris and had its fuse underneath; with the help of McFetridge and Novis the debris was cleared very carefully, the mine turned over and access gained to the fuse and successfully rendered safe. It was a most creditable performance for the first mine as this was a difficult one requiring quiet nerve and application.

Later in December he dealt with two mines at Romford, Essex, which was attended with only normal risks but on looking into the inspection hole for the two common signs he considered that these mines had a unit which was unusual. The mines were sent for complete investigation and found to contain a new type of magnetic unit, the discovery of which was of the utmost importance.

On 4th January 1941 a mine was buried in the basement of a house in Ninian Park, Cardiff near the railway. Helped by A.B. Mountford he first had to clear the entire debris etc and pull the mine out so that it could be dismantled. The actual removal of the bomb fuse had to be done in situ, by hand, as that it could be done form a safe distance.

This officer showed a high degree of courage and coolness in rendering it safe.

On the 14th December 1940, John McFetridge, helped Lieutenant Kessack to clear debris from a mine which had fallen in a clubroom at Birmingham.

The bomb fuse was underneath and particular care was needed to turn an active and dangerous mine to reach the fuse; a very dangerous operation.

On 3rd January 1941, he helped Sub-Lieutenant Reid to dispose of a particularly difficult mine in Cardiff. The arrangements for getting the mine out of the spot in which it was buried called for great ingenuity and courage. He was a great help, regardless of the attendant dangers.

Extract from "Report on Mines Laid on Land, 9th January 1941 to 30th November 1941" By Admiral H Phillips DMT.

It is regretted to report that on 28th April 1941 Lieutenant J.H.H Kessack, GM lost his life while attempting to render a mine safe. Kessack was an experienced officer who had dealt already with twenty-seven mines and had been recommended for high awards. The mine that killed him was 'lying pretty' and was apparently a normal one. His death emphasises that, in spite of improved techniques, that act of rendering a mine safe is still extremely dangerous as any mine may blow up on being approached or in the course of operations. This also emphasised by a case which occurred at Cardross Railway Station, Dumbarton, Glasgow on the 6th May where Sub-Lieutenant John Mill, RNVR only just escaped with his life".

Mid December 1940

George Medal: Howard Dudley Reid, Lieutenant Royal Australian Naval Volunteer Reserve, Mine Disposal.

London Gazette 27/6/1941

He has dealt successfully with six unexploded enemy mines and has shown constant courage of the highest degree, ingenuity and persistence.

In mid-December 1940, in Birmingham he was rendering a mine safe and whilst dealing with it the bomb fuse clock started, but he returned to it and finished the operation successfully.

On 3rd January 1941 a mine fell Crawshay Lane, Cardiff very near to Messrs, Curran's works, the Central Railway Station and a Freezing Works; the parachute of this mine had failed, consequently it had fallen with terrific force and buried itself in a pavement, in doing so it had severed a water main and electric power cable. The impossibility of removing this mine quickly and preventing it exploding was apparent. By the end of the day the water had been removed from the hole and great ingenuity had been shown with the aid of ropes, locks, lamp posts, etc. to haul the mine out by its parachute cords with a lorry, unfortunately only the parachute came away as its attachment had been damaged. McFetridge and A.B. Tuckwell, GC were helping on the evening of 4th January with everything frozen hard, Reid got into the hole, broke up the hard ground and exposed the base of the mine. It was then thought that the mine might be broken up but a little more excavation proved it to be intact and dangerous. A new parachute attachment from another better rig, and mine, which had been rendered safe was fitted to haul the mine out. This was successful and Reid after carefully cleaning the bomb fuse with a toothbrush fitted the safety gag while the mine was still suspended. The mine looked as if all was well but the bomb fuse could not be shifted owing to damage, all tools got bent or broken. Special new ones were made in Curran's works, the safety gag kept on getting displaced and then the bomb fuse started. After a time Reid returned to find that the gag was very much displaced, the bomb fuse being very likely to fire at once, if any more displacement occurred. Nevertheless, on 5th January, with the aid of a specially made tool. Reid at last succeeded in removing the fuse. It was then found that owing to damage to the mine it was impossible to remove the primer and detonator so that in order to get the mine was it was put on a lorry and carefully removed to a suitable site and boiled out.

Incidents: 9th October, 9th November and 16th December 1940.

George Medal: William Suttle, 1883145 Acting Lance Corporal Royal Engineers, 9th Bomb Disposal Company.

London Gazette 30/9/1941
9th October 1940, in Stafford, a 250-Kilogram bomb fell in the Test Laboratory and Transfer House of English Electric Company at 11am. It was found with a 17 and a 50-type fuse, the 17 fuse ticking. The party arrived on the spot at approximately 3.30pm and the 17 fuse was immobilised remotely by the Officer n charge. It was not found possible to remove the 50-fuse at the base plate. At that time there was no appliance for dealing with the 50 fuse and the only course open was to remove the bomb very gently to a site approximately two hundred yards away. Lance Corporal Suttle volunteered for the job, which was successfully completed by 4.30pm.

9th November 1940, in Coventry, two bobs fell at the Aeroplane Assembly Shop of the Humber Hillman Factory; both were diagnosed as 250 kilogram and were approximately seventy yards apart. During the morning, one exploded, killing two of the working party. Suttle was in charge of the party at the second bomb and volunteered to remain at the job. His courage and determined resource resulted in the successful removal of the second bomb, which turned out to be a 1,000-kilogram device, at 3pm the same day.

14th December 1940, in Birmingham, Whilst working on a suspended unexploded bomb at Olton Boulevard, a crater was encountered, one man fell into the crater and was immediately overcome by fumes. Suttle immediately fastened a rope about himself and descended into the crater. He secured the unconscious man with rope left in the hole for the purpose and refused to be drawn up until the first man had been extricated. When he was drawn to the surface he was also found to be suffering from the effects of gas.

Incidents August, October and December 1940

British Empire Medal: Harold Wood, Police Sergeant, 20 Old Farm Road, Stechford Birmingham.

London Gazette 11/7/1941

During air raids, Sergeant Harold Wood had proved himself capable and efficient, and has shown great devoting to duty. He is always willing and anxious to attend at any incidents, which occur, and his actions have given encouragement and confidence to the constables, wardens and others who rendered assistance at incidents.

On the night of the 14th August 1940, he assisted during a heavy air attack. He was sent out to take charge of an incident at Yardley Trust Almshouses, Church Road, Yardley. Nine high explosive bombs had been dropped in the vicinity of these almshouses, several of them being reported as unexploded. A number of Wardens and civilians, about 30 in all, were present, and the Sergeant arranged for the disposition of these, and searched for the unexploded bombs. Inmates of the almshouses

Sergt. H. E. Wood

were accommodated in the Yardley Schools, and many of them, who were aged women, were seriously distressed, some almost on the point of collapse. Sergeant Wood visited them at the school from time to time during the raid with the help of two or three women managed to encourage and calm them. Wood was engaged as Incident officer for nearly eight hours.

On the 16th August 1940, many incendiary fires were started in the vicinity of Station Road, Stechford. There were so many fires that the Auxiliary Fire Service (AFS) were fully engaged and still there were many fires unattended. Sergeant Wood borrowed two canvas buckets and a shovel form the fire brigade and went himself to about 14 houses, which were on fire. In some of these he found incendiaries had penetrated the roof to the bedroom floor and he was able in some cases to shovel the incendiary bomb through the window into the garden below, afterwards dealing with the outbreaks of fire with buckets of water. Eventually additional AFS pumps arrived and Wood directed these to the more serious fires in the district.

On the 26th August 1940, at 8.30am Sergeant Wood was told there was a suspected delayed action bomb in a yard adjoining 55 Lichfield Road, Aston. There was evidence of the presence there of an unexploded bomb and Wood commenced to evacuate the residents in the vicinity and in some cases had to visit bedrooms to get elderly people to come from their beds. At about 9am the owner of this yard arrived and informed the Sergeant that the bomb must be resting either in or very near two tanks, one containing petrol and the other oil. Wood summoned the fire brigade to stand by and extended the evacuation area, which then included much factory property and involved tramway and omnibus services. Wood then obtained a plan of the yard from the owner and marked upon it the location of the tanks, and this he gave to Lieutenant Rayner of the Bomb Disposal Section, on his arrival to inspect the site. In due course the Bomb Disposal Section removed from the site one delayed action bomb of 500 lbs weight.

On the 15th October 1940, Sergeant Wood was patrolling in Aston Church Road when an air attack commenced and bombs began to fall in the grounds around the Nechells Power Station. Sergeant Wood was informed that several bombs had failed to explode on impact. He learned from an observer at the Power Station that one unexploded bomb had fallen near the main London, Midland and Scottish Railway Companies line, that runs to Derby and the north, which runs along the edge of this ground where it joins the Tame and the Rea Drainage Board Workings. He at once informed the Central Railway Control, Saltley, by telephone in order to stop railway traffic pending further examination. With a special constable and several employees of the Nechells Power Station, Sergeant Wood commenced a search of the whole of this ground and whilst this was going on aircraft were overhead and further high explosive bombs were dropped. Soon afterwards the men from the Power Station left the search party and the Special Constable and Wood continued alone. When near to the office and stables of the Tame and Rea Drainage Board, two high explosive bombs fell and one of them demolished the stables and tore up the railway track within the grounds. The other bomb fractured the main water supply to the Drainage Board and badly damaged the offices. The blast from these bombs was felt by Sergeant Wood who was showered with debris. He went into the offices, found them unoccupied and that the men on duty there had gone to a nearby shelter. In the stables he found a horse partially buried and with one end of the roof holding it down. He called for a Rescue Squad to extricate the horse, but immediately after their arrival this squad received a call to a house where there were people trapped, and the horse was left. With the assistance of some workmen, Sergeant Wood placed supports between the floor and roof to keep the weight off the horse and sent for a veterinary surgeon. The horse was rescued unhurt on the following day. Sergeant Wood posted employees of the Drainage Board at all entrances to the ground to keep workmen and others from the area where unexploded bombs had fallen. He was engaged in this area throughout the whole raid and for about six and a half hours and almost continuously bombs were falling and there was heavy gunfire.

17th October 1940, a bomb fell into the premises of the Metropolitan-Cammell Carriage & Wagon Works. Wood could see a large fire had started in the offices at these works. He assisted in getting fire pumps through to the water supply form the Gas Works. During this time high explosive bombs were being dropped in many other streets in this vicinity and Sergeant Wood cycled round the district visiting the scene of the incidents and checking the steps taken by the various incident officers and assisting in whatever way he found possible.

18th October 1940, Sergeant Wood was at Bloomsbury Street Police Station when he heard a heavy explosion close by. He saw flames coming from Bennetts Garage, Great Lister Street. There were two men, members of the Home Guard lying on the footway opposite. He sent a messenger to the Lingard Street Fire Station and ran himself to the police station and asked for two ambulances to be sent and asked that the Fire Control should be informed that it was a serious fire. Sergeant Wood returned to the scene and was then informed by his messenger that the Fire Brigade had no one to send. The fires were spreading and the flames were at this time 50 feet high. He sent to the Fire Station for hose, stand pipes and hydrant keys and whilst these were being brought he located the water supply and had the hydrants uncovered ready for action. Four standpipes with hoses were set up and four jets were soon at work, two at the front and two at the rear of the fire. Sergeant Wood directed ARP Wardens and civilians to concentrate on preventing the fire spreading to adjoining houses and shops. Tanks of the cars in the garage were bursting and there were petrol pumps along the front of the garage and the pipes of these were alight and jets of petrol on fire coming out. Soon after a fireman with tender, also the AFS came to the scene and took charge of the fire, whilst he dealt with the damage. Many high explosive bombs were dropped in the vicinity during the time and one demolished a garage and blew a car out of the garage over a wall into the next street were it remained overturned in the middle of the road. The blast from this bomb blew flames out from the fire to where Wood was lying in the road and quantities of debris fell around him. The whole of Great Lister Street, for about 150 yards, was badly damaged by the bomb which started the fire, and the Bank premises, a post Office, were open, the shutters of a jewellers had been torn away exposing diamond rings, gold watches and other jewellery, some of which was scattered about the street. Many other shops were also blown open and Wood obtained the services of the Home Guard to mount guard over this property.

25th October 1940, at 9pm an incident occurred at the junction of Dartmouth Street and Great Lister Street, and also on inside the premises of the Delta Metal Co Ltd. Dartmouth Street. There were 12 casualties at these two incidents and Sergeant Wood went there and took charge as Incident Officer. The presence of a delayed action bomb near the Delta Factory was reported. A Corporation omnibus and an AFS pump had been involved and both drivers had been taken to hospital. These vehicles were standing very near to the suspected delayed action bomb and after dealing with evacuation, he decided to try to move these vehicles to save them from complete destruction should the bomb explode. The pump was a new one of the large type and was not very badly damaged and he was able to start up the engine and drive it to Lister Street to greater safety. The engine of the omnibus was damaged and he was unable to move this vehicle.

On Tuesday, 3rd December 1940, incidents were reported in the Witton District and at the premises of the General Electric Co. Messrs Hardy Spicers Ltd. Also at a house in Brantley Road, Witton. Wood attended at these incidents, also in Cheshire Road and Deykin Avenue, and arranged for the attendance of the necessary Services, etc. There was much air activity in this area and many bombs were falling nearby.

On Wednesday, 4th December 1940, at 8pm Sergeant Wood went to the Manor Road district of Aston, Where a number of high explosive bombs had been dropped causing considerable damage. There were 18 casualties and many people were homeless. He took charge of the area and co-ordinated the services, arranged transport for the injured and for aged people rendered homeless to the Reception Depot. About 100 people had to leave their homes and the Sergeant supplied the necessary billeting forms. He also examined the site of a reported delayed action bomb on the LM&S Railway branch line to Walsall, and informed the Railway Control so that rail traffic could be stopped over this section of the line. Large number of shops had been damaged and the stocks there were exposed and the sergeant obtained the assistance of members of he Home Guard for the protection of this property. The overhead tram wires in Witton Lane were broken down and he took steps to see that this was quickly attended to.

Incidents October to February 1940

British Empire Medal: Walter James Langley, Temporary Police Sergeant. London Gazette 11/7/1941

Sergeant Langley has displayed great resource, energy and courage in dealing with air attack incidents, rescuing trapped persons and taking the necessary precautions with respect to unexploded bombs. Of twenty-four air attack incidents in which he was concerned, which illustrates his energy and praiseworthy conduct. It will be noted that nine air raids are concerned and that on the night, 19th November 1940 he attended seven separate incidents.

On the 15th October 1940, in St Lukes Road, delayed action bomb had fallen on the rear of the house and buried itself in the cellar. He found two elderly persons in the house, one of whom was trapped beneath fallen masonry. He extricated this person and rendered first aid. About ten minutes later the bomb exploded demolishing this dwelling house and the one next door. At the same time a high explosive bomb fell on the Jewish School, St Lukes Road. He attended and found that the two upper rooms of the school were severely damaged. Underneath the building was a public shelter in which a number of people were sheltering. He advised the occupants that as the shelter had not been damaged in any way it was better for them to remain where they were as bombs were falling in the vicinity.

On 18th October 1940, in Gough Road, Edgbaston, a high explosive bomb fell on a house, Langley found five persons had been trapped in the cellar. It was not possible to rescue these trapped persons owning to the amount of debris, but a hole was made through which a Doctor assisted by Langley, was able to reach the trapped people, and inject morphia to the injured persons who were released the following morning.

On 25th October 1940, in Bellbarn Road, a high explosive bomb fell on houses, which were demolished. Langley made enquiries and was informed that one person was missing. He continued his enquiries and was successful in tracing the man. He later took persons rendered homeless to a Rest Centre.

On 26th October 1940, in Grosvenor Street West and Sheepcote Street, a high explosive bomb fell demolishing four houses. One woman was trapped beneath the debris and Langley assisted the Rescue Squad in extricating her. It was found that a man was in the attic of a partly demolished house and Sergeant Langley assisted him to safety. In Sheepcote Street, a large crater had been formed in the carriageway and gas and water mains were damaged. With the assistance of a bystander he descended the crater and reduced the escape of gas by plugging the fracture with mud. He obtained ropes and lamps round the crater.

On 5th November 1940, in Oozells Street, Stoke Street and Wheeleys Lane an oil bomb fell on Messers Wales Ltd. Oozells Street and an high explosive bomb fell in the roadway damaging the gas main, igniting the gas. He organised Wardens and then assisted the firms Fire Brigade in operating a jet on their burning building and prevented the fire from spreading. In Stoke Street several houses had been damaged by a high explosive bomb. He assisted the Rescue Squad in extricating some trapped persons. The damaged houses were very old and there was a great deal of danger from falling masonry. Several high explosive bombs had partially demolished a factory and some houses in Wheeleys Lane. He found a number of people had been rendered homeless, these he escorted to a Rest Centre.

On 19th November 1940, in Viceroy Close, two motor cars were burning inside a large garage and he endeavoured to extinguish the fire with sand and buckets of water. Whilst doing this a petrol tank exploded and Langley was slightly shocked. The fire was eventually extinguished. In Wellington Road, a high explosive bomb had demolished a house. A man was trapped beneath the debris and a large water pipe was fractured, the water escaping into the cellar in which the man was trapped. With assistance he rescued the trapped man, after which he plugged the water pipe. In Alexandra Road, several houses had been demolished and a woman was trapped in a room, which was partially demolished. He was able to rescue her and when doing so a quantity of masonry fell near him. In Bristol Road, five persons were trapped in a cellar of a house, which had been demolished. A Rescue Squad was at work and he assisted and advised them. The trapped persons could not be rescued at that time, but it was possible to pass them stimulants; these persons being rescued the following day. In Pershore Road, a high explosive bomb fell on houses and shops demolishing parts of them. Several people were suffering shock and he rendered first aid. In Belgrave Road, a high explosive bomb had demolished a number of houses. Langley found one woman was trapped in the cellar, who was suffering form head injuries. He was successful in getting her out, treated her for superficial injuries and left her in the care of friends. Langley, finally assisted at the Police Club, Tally Ho Grounds, Pershore Road. where, he and a number of Special Constables aided the AFS, who were hampered by lack of water and proved unable to prevent severe damage to the pavilion.

On the 22nd November 1940, in Bellis Street, Ladywood, a number of incendiaries and a high explosive bomb caused much damage to houses and a cinema. Langley attended with other officers and conducted the homeless to a Rest Centre, prior to this he assisted to extinguish a number of small fires in St Vincent Street, Ladywood. In Friston Street, Ladywood, four houses were demolished by a high explosive bomb and a number of people were trapped. Assisted by other police officers he commenced to remove debris in order to extricate the trapped persons. He descended a cellar and found that a gas main had been fractured and there was a fire. One man was extracted after which Langley found it necessary to timber up the cellar to prevent the fall of debris. Rescue work was then continued and another man who had sustained a fractured femur was extricated. During the rescue work debris was falling continually but by constant efforts seven persons were rescued. Temp

Sergeant Langley together with other officers were engaged in this incident for eight hours under difficult circumstances owing to lack of light, escaping gas and the close proximity of an electric cable which had been damaged. In Sherbourne Street, houses had been demolished by a high explosive bomb. He assisted in the rescue work releasing a number of persons.

On 11th December 1940, in St James Road and Frederick Road, Edgbaston, delayed action bombs were reported in the vicinity of these roads. Langley located the places where these bombs had fallen and found that they had exploded. In Arthur Road, Edgbaston, a high explosive bomb had fallen in the roadway at the junction with Edgbaston Park Road. He arranged for traffic to be diverted and then made search for casualties. A delayed action bomb had fallen in the vicinity and he organised a search party. In Sun Street West, a high explosive bomb partially demolished a factory. Langley organised the traffic; he then obtained the services of a Home Guard to post sentry at the premises. A number of houses were damaged, the occupiers in their endeavour to get away had left lights burning, Langley then entered the premises to extinguish them, and searched for casualties. He then rendered first aid to a number of people who had sustained minor injuries.

On the 1st February 1941, in Pershore Road, Edgbaston, Sergeant Langley was on duty when he heard something falling in the vicinity. He made a thorough search of fields and waste ground to discover what had fallen. But he was unable at the time, due to the darkness, to discover the location of what later turned out to be a parachute mine.

Incidents October, November and December 1940

British Empire Medal: Harold Whittall, Police Inspector C Division[1].

London Gazette 11/7/1941

Throughout the various raids on the Handsworth district, Inspector Whittall has always displayed a cheerful demeanour to everyone under him, and to the other services working in conjunction with the police. In addition he has never spared himself, working long hours and subjecting himself to all the dangers consequent upon exposure to attacks from the air, and his conduct throughout is deserving of the highest commendation. The following are extracts from the recommendation.

On Sunday 27th October 1940, a number of incendiary bombs fell in Brewery Street, Holyhead Road, Sycamore Road, Queens Head Road, Boulton Road and other streets near Holyhead Police Station, where Inspector Whittall is stationed. Air Raid Wardens and Police co-operated in extinguishing these bombs, which was done with remarkable speed. Whittall not only organised parties to deal with these bombs, but also personally dealt with several himself and by his actions, inspired others.

---

[1] *There is a photo of Inspector Whittall in the, Birmingham Gazette, 12/7/1941, page. 3.*

On Monday 28th October 1940, as on the previous occasion, numbers of incendiary bombs were dropped in the Handsworth district, but in a much wider area. A great number of incendiaries were dropped in streets in all parts of the section. As on the former occasion, Inspector Whittall assisted in dealing with the bombs himself, in addition to organising the fire parties.

On Tuesday 19th November 1940, the district was subjected to heavy bombing, high explosive, delayed action and incendiary bombs falling in almost every part of the Handsworth sub-section. Gas and electric services were interfered with in many cases, and in several instances traffic was seriously affected. Bombing commenced at 6.50pm and continued for nearly ten hours. Very considerable damage was caused to property in the district and in several cases persons were buried in the ruins of their own homes. Whittall organised the work of the police and personally visited several of the more serious incidents and assisted in the work of rescue. He visited Murdock Road, where two persons were rescued and one body recovered from the debris. The heavy bombing that Handsworth and district was subjected to on this occasion taxed the police strength to its utmost, and Inspector Whittall considered it necessary to call on other stations on the division for assistance.

On Saturday 23rd November 1940, a large number of high explosive, delayed action and incendiary bombs fell in the Handsworth district. There were major incidents in Grove Hill Road, Farnham Road, Thornhill Road, Yorks Road, and Downing Street. In all these cases serious damage was done. In addition to the above, high explosive, delayed action and incendiary bombs fell in nine other streets in Handsworth and high explosive in Handsworth Park and on the golf course. Incendiary bombs fell and set fire to the premises of Messrs Evans & Evans, Soho Road, completely gutting it and on the factory of Messrs Bloxidge Brothers, Holliday Road.

Inspector Whittall organised the police work at all to the above incidents and as on 19th November 1940, he found it necessary to appeal for assistance and constables were sent to other stations on the division. He did not spare himself at all and personally visited all the more important incidents and a number of the others, and personally supervised the work of the police. On this occasion, explosive incendiary bombs were used by the enemy and a number of persons were injured in attempting to put out these bombs and this greatly added to the work of the police. Whittall himself extinguished several of these bombs and gave valuable advice as to the best approach to them.

A bomb crater was discovered a few feet from the explosive magazine at the Jubilee Pit and the police were informed. A large quantity of explosives is kept at this magazine and the possibilities of damage if a bomb exploded a few feet away was great. Whittall attended at once and with the manager examined the crater. They satisfied themselves that the bomb had already exploded. Work of this nature must of necessity be attended with grave personal risk, but the Inspector regarded it as his duty.

On Wednesday 11th December 1940, during the night of the 11th and 12th December in which five parachute mines fell in the Handsworth area, in addition to which several high explosive bombs were dropped in the district. Widespread damage was caused and there were a number of fatal and living casualties. A large number of persons were rendered homeless. In the case of the parachute mine which exploded in Albert Road, Douglas Road and Charles Street, it was necessary for the police to find immediate shelter for these persons rendered homeless and these arrangements were carried out with the least possible delay by Inspector Whittall and the men under his command. He visited each incident. In the case of the mine in Charles Street, which fell in the GWR goods yard, three members of the Company's Home Guard were killed and several horses were also killed. The inspector immediately attended on receiving the report and made a personal examination of the premises and directed the assistance given by the police. In addition to the above parachute mines which exploded on impact, two unexploded mines fell in the Handsworth district, one at the rear of 28 Queens Head Road and one in the allotments at the junction of Friary Road and Oxhill Road, at the other side of the section. In the case of the mine in Queens Head Road, this exploded in the afternoon of the 12th December, when being removed by the Naval Authorities. The one in Friary Road was successfully removed, without incident, on the 14th. In both cases it was necessary to evacuate a large number of people over a wide area, and this was done with the ever-possible risk of the mines exploding. Inspector Whittall visited both mines and personally supervised the evacuation. He displayed great courage and personal disregard to danger in this work.

1940

British Empire Medal: Kenneth Ashton, 1914139 Lance Corporal (Acting Corporal) Royal Engineers, 9 Bomb Disposal Company.

London Gazette 1/7/1941
This award appears in the Birthday Honours of the London Gazette's without citation. However, Kenneth Ashton was engaged in bomb disposal duties over a period of times, and whilst no citation or recommendation papers have been traced, this award in undoubtedly for gallantry.

Raid 9th April 1941

British Empire Medal: Thomas Bradley, ARP Warden.
King's Commendation: Arthur Pain, ARP Warden; Eric Warden Copson, ARP Warden.

London Gazette 20/6/1941

At 9.55, on Wednesday, April 9th 1941, an "Alert" sounded and Bradley left his house to patrol his sector. At about 10.45pm he heard two or three heavy bombs fall in Washwood Heath Road vicinity and thinking that the wardens' post had been struck he ran there to render assistance.

He arrived to see the Post Warden Mr C.P. Brown being carried into the post by two wardens. Brown had been standing in Washwood Heath Road, and was struck by bomb splinters, which caused a very severe lacerated wound to the left arm, and wounds to the head, face and chest.

Bradley diagnosed arterial bleeding form the wound in the arm and instructed Miss Richards, a paid Warden to apply digital pressure to the left sub-clavian artery whilst he dressed the wound and applied a tourniquet. Whilst doing this, more bombs fell in the vicinity and the window at the post was broken, the black out fell down and the electric light failed. Bradley carried on by the light of a hurricane lamp. Miss Richards and Mrs Sowell the paid Wardens on duty have stated it was a terrifying experience, but Bradley carried on without any apparent fear.

There is no doubt that Bradley by his prompt and efficient first aid under trying circumstances saved the life of Brown, who was in a state of collapse due to loss of blood.

After seeing Brown in the ambulance Bradley returned to his sector and at about 1.00am a heavy bomb fell in St Margaret's Road near Bromford Lane. It demolished an Off-Licence Beer House occupied by a Mr and Mrs Payton, and the house next door. Bradley ran there and ascertained from neighbours that the Payton's were trapped in the cellar. Bradley knew that his Deputy Group Warden had gone to report the incident but he ran to the post to report the casualties.

He there learned that the telephone was out of order and went back to organise the rescue. He found other Wardens Mr Copson and Mr Pain removing debris. Bradley got the assistance of others[1] and cleared a way. While bombs were falling they had to break a way in with great difficulty and got out a very stout woman alive. They cleared a way to the buried man, and kept him alive until the Rescue Party arrived to get him clear of the ruins. During their labours coal gas was present in the cellar.

Bradley saved three lives, and his bravery and devotion to duty are worthy of recognition.

---

[1] *The "others" included warden Alfred Brewin, who assisted in the rescue despite being injured by the bomb which caused the destruction of the off licence.*

Raid 9th April 1941

King's Commendation: T McIntyre, Private 25th Birmingham Battalion Home Guard. [later 45th Warwickshire (Birmingham) Battalion Home Guard][1]

History of 45th Warwickshire (Birmingham) Battalion Home Guard, by Lieutenant Colonel Barclay

On the night of April 9th 1941, there was another heavy blitz. The Squad on duty at Brearley Street Works that night consisted of Captain Brown; Lance Corporal Johnson and Privates, J Ashberry, T Hamilton, B Jones, W Smith and T McIntyre.

The works of E Elliott Ltd. Summer Lane received a direct hit from a high explosive bomb, and the Squad acted with great promptitude and efficiency, manning the trailer pump for one and a half hours, and keeping the fire under control until the Auxiliary Fire Service arrived on the scene.

During this incident, great heroism was shown by Private McIntyre; who at very great risk to himself from falling masonry, rescued a number of people who were trapped. He later received a Certificate of Commendation from His Majesty the King.

Raid 9th to 10th April 1941

George Medal: Ronald Jackson, Probationary Police Constable 335.E[2]

London Gazette 6/6/1941

On the night of the 9th to the 10th April 1941, high explosive bombs demolished some flats in Garrison Lane, to the rear of the Birmingham City Football Clubs ground. Parts of the concrete floor fell across a bed on which a woman was lying. The Wardens had succeeded in removing some of the concrete from the woman's chest, but she was still trapped form the waist downwards. It was considered too dangerous to remove any more debris, as there was every possibility of the remainder of the ceiling falling.

Ronald Jackson then went to the rear of the building and attacked the wreckage from the outside. He succeeded in burrowing through and reached the fallen masonry, which was pinning the casualty. Lying in water from burst pipes he commenced sawing through the concrete and after working alone for two hours he succeeded in freeing the injured woman.

Jackson showed great courage and gallantry, being fully aware that the remainder of the building might collapse at any moment.

---

[1] *London Gazette 28/11/1941.*
[2] *His George Medal is in the possession of the Birmingham Constabulary.*

Birmingham Evening Mail 5th January, 1970

The first policeman in Birmingham to win the George Medal is soon leaving the force. Chief Inspector Ronald Jackson, head of the Fingerprint Department of Birmingham City Police, retires next week. He was awarded the George Medal in 1941 for rescuing a woman trapped in the debris of a bombed block of flats, in Garrison Lane, Small Heath. King George VI, who had established the award the previous year as a recognition of acts of gallantry, presented it to him at Buckingham Palace.

Today Mr Jackson, whose father was a sergeant in Dewsbury Borough Police, has a son serving as a police constable near where he won his medal. He works for Bordesley Green Police Station.

It was in 1942 that Chief Inspector Jackson started his 28 years service in the CID. He joined the fingerprint department in 1946 and became its head in 1960. He played a major role in the formation of the Midland Criminal Records Office, which holds more than 1,000,000 fingerprints on Midland criminals; a collection growing at a rate of 13.000 a year.

Raid 9th to 10th April 1941

The Award of the George Medal (GM): to Arthur John Rycroft; Chief Inspector - London, Midland & Scottish Railway.

London Gazette 8th August 1941

In the marshalling yard of Washwood Heath sidings wagons were being sorted when the air raid started. Incendiaries fell and were exploding over the area starting fires in some of the coal and coke wagons, then one went through the wooden roof of a van containing cordite and the top of the wagon was soon on fire. Inspector Freeman made the first attempt to tackle this, he got within 75 yards when explosions began to take place in the middle of a shunt of seven wagons, all containing explosives.

In was impossible to get sufficient water to the wagon, so it was decided to isolate the burning wagon with a shunting engine. To clear the burning wagon it was necessary to uncouple it from other munitions wagons in front and behind. Chief Inspector Rycroft

Arthur John Rycroft

did this himself, actually going under the exploding wagon, the undercarriage and couplings of which were already hot. While he was doing this, Guard Bull coupled the forward munitions wagon on to a large shunt, which was drawn by a light engine, to a distant siding. The same was done on the other side. Left to itself the cordite wagon eventually blew up and burned out. Meanwhile, a wagon was alight on another line near the burning cordite, Rycroft climbed to the top of the wagon to fight the fire when part of the burning cordite blew him to the ground. As the night wore on the lighted wagons attracted heavy bombing and casualties were occurring throughout the control area. Nine burning wagons of coal and coke were unloaded and two wagonloads of pigs, threatened by fire, were detached and shunted to a quiet area. After a lull, the sound of a bomb dropping on the line sent the two inspectors to investigate, they found a locomotive fireman who had been struck on the back of the head and there was a man who needed assistance in a shelter. Rycroft went on foot to the nearest Police post and was promised an ambulance, if one of the injured men could be carried to a point two miles from the shelter by stretcher. Rycroft and Freeman carried the stretcher with the injured man on it along the line with the less injured man walking with them. They had to pass between two large warehouse fires. An army lorry took the wounded men to hospital.

From: Heroes of Road and Rail[1]

I sat in an office on the outer perimeter of Birmingham talking with L.M.S District controller Garfield, about blitz nights, and particularly one in 1941. Outside goods trains were continually on the move. Engines large and small were pulling and pushing great wagons loaded up to 20 tons each; shunters were coupling and uncoupling; signalmen taking and transmitting order.

Our talk turned at first on the work of goods yards. "Since Hamm." Said Mr Garfield, with a smile, "the public understand better the term 'marshalling' yard, which best describes the work that has to be done here. Trains come in from every direction bringing all kinds of goods-food, coal and coke, petrol, war supplies. These have to be sorted out in the sidings and made up into fresh trains to be passed on to their final destinations. After a big blitz things may be in a good deal of a mess, but we have our plans worked out, not only for repairing damage, but for seeing that the work goes on without interruption-or with as little as possible.

After a very bad night 168 bomb craters were counted in one marshalling yard, and 50 major interruptions were notified on the line, bringing a call for immediate action affecting eight separate sections of railroad organisation. Each of these sections is normally in close contract with the others by telephone. The time all communication was cut, and had to be brought into line again. There were nights when no engine could move, or car to take a messenger.

"And yet, so complete was our emergency organisation that it was possible for each department to restore complete working within a few hours. Trains had to be

---

1 CURNOCK G.C. Heroes of Road and Rail (Simpkin Marshall Ltd, London, 1941) p, 7782.
There is a picture of Arthur Rycroft, on page 76.

diverted at considerable distances in the meantime, but we never had an accident of any kind, and foods and passengers arrived safely at their destinations, whether cities, camps, factories or depots. Whatever happens, the rail men manage to do their part in keeping the war wheels turning".

I looked out of the window across a broad stretch of interlacing rail tracks. No trace of Jerry's handiwork was to be seen here.

Asked for an example of some damages the Controller had to clear up, he said: "You see that bridge, 50 or 60 yards from us towards the right? One night Jerry dropped a 200lb. Bomb plumb in the middle of two of the seven roads that cross it. It was the biggest shake-up this building had. I went out to see what mischief had been done. It was an amazing sight! The bomb, which must have come from a fabulous height, had made a clean hole through the bridge, and continuing its vertical drive, penetrated the road below.

"Where the explosion took place. The result was almost unbelievable. At the moment of the explosion an engine and tender were standing on the bridge. By blast only, coming from such a confined space, girders were torn out of their bed-plates and lifted at an acute angle, with the engine and tender remaining on the rail they carried!

"Our main concern at the moment was to save the engine. It was in danger of falling through the hole to the road below. We hitched up another engine, and by degrees managed to lug her back on to a flat road again.

"Six of the seven roads were put out of action for the time being, but we were able to keep one working and the rest were back to normal before very long"

This was a bad night but the marshalling yard's worst night was that in which Chief Inspector Arthur Rycroft won his George Medal for courage, devotion to duty, and leadership and five who aided in the fight with the Hun on a clear moon-lit night received commendations.

Wagons were being sorted and remade into trains. Planes began circling about 9.45; distant flashes and sounds showed what might be expected. Satisfied that all was ready for action if need be, Rycroft, an old soldier of the last war, 46 years old, with 31 years L.M.S service, went on with his marshalling.

Incendiaries soon were cracking, whirling and exploding all over the area. Fires started in some of the coal and coke wagons. First attention was paid to these. Then one went through the wooden roof of a van containing cordite and the top of the van was soon on fire.

Inspector Freeman made the first attempt to tackle this danger. He got within 75 yards, when explosions began to take place in the middle of a shunt of 7 wagons, all containing explosives, and this is what he saw:

"Each reel of cordite was exploding in turn as the fire reached it. The blast was going 'Phit-phit' and sending out millions of sparks. Cordite has a great forcing power. It was belching everywhere through the roof and sides, and threatening wagons all round.

"It was impossible to get sufficient water to the wagon, so I decided to see what could be done to isolate the burning wagon with a shunting engine. At that moment Chief Inspector Rycroft came down the yard.

"He got down to the job at once. To clear the burning wagon it was necessary to uncouple it from other munitions wagon in front and behind. This Rycroft did himself, actually going under the exploding wagon, the undercarriage and couplings of which were already hot. While he was doing this, Guard Bull coupled the forward munitions wagons on to a large shunt of 35 wagons which, drawn by a light engine, took them to a distant siding. The same was done on the other side. Left to itself the cordite wagons eventually blew up and burned out".

This was not the end of the adventure with the burning wagon. A potato wagon was alight on another line near the cordite furnace. Rycroft climbed to the top of the wagon and was getting a stirrup-pump nozzle into the cavity of the roof when an extra burst on the part of the burning cordite blew him to the ground.

Asked what it felt like to be blasted from a potato van by cordite explosion, the Inspector gave a characteristic reply: "Don't say I was blown off; better say I tumbled off. I think that's nearer the mark".

As this night wore on there were many grimmer incidents in the L.M.S. sidings. The lighted wagons attracted the "heavy stuff" and casualties were occurring throughout the control area. Nine burning wagons of coal and coke were unloaded. A new wave of incendiaries falling upon the yard, Rycroft's corps of 20 men 'threw anything we could get on them, including slack coal'! Two wagonloads of pigs, threatened by fire, were detached and shunted to a quiet corner.

After "a bit of a lull" the sound of a bomb dropping on the line sent the two inspectors "to see what was happening". Freeman, who has spent most of his leisure in St. John Ambulance work, found a locomotive fireman in a bad way. He had been relieved from duty and was walking to "sign of" when he was struck on the back of the head. As soon as his head was bound up the man told them that there was a man who wanted help in shelter. They found two very badly injured. An ambulance was wanted. Rycroft himself went on foot to the nearest Police post, only to be reached by a perilous passage between two great warehouse fires. Reaching the post, he was promised that an ambulance would be sent to take at least one of the victims if he could be carried to a point two miles from the shelter by stretcher. Dashing back throughout the fire, the chief inspector, with the aid of Inspector Freeman, manned the stretcher and made the journey on foot along the line, the less injured man walking with them. The promised ambulance failing to arrive, an army lorry took its place, and the wounded men at last reached the hospital.

Raid 9th to 10th April 1941

The award of the British Empire Medal (BEM): Mrs Amelia Johnson, A.R.P Warden. And the King's Commendation (KC) to; Charles Baker 190 Bradford Street, Fire Watcher; William McGinn Carter, 52 Ravenhurst Street, A.R.P Warden and Maurice Stather, Constable E.201, Moseley Street Police Station.

London Gazette 7/7/1941

At 01.10 hours on 10th April 1941, during an air attack on the city a H.E bomb fell on houses 101 and 102 Ravenhurst Street, Camp Hill, demolishing same and trapping eight persons in the debris. Mrs Johnson was on patrol and at once went to the First Aid Post at the Rowton House to get assistance. Other H.E bombs fell in the vicinity whilst she was on the way there were factory fires and gas mains had been ignited. She reached the Post and secured the services of Dr H. Middleton Turnbull[1], but on returning to the incident found Moseley Street was blocked and they went by another route. Mrs Johnson endeavoured to get through the debris into the cellar of one of the wrecked houses, but was unable to do so, and leaving the Doctor at the scene, she went back to Moseley Street Police Station where proper rescue work was organised, and Mrs Johnson then went back to the incident, where she assisted in attending to four living casualties who had been rescued. Two bodies had also been got out, and two more bodies were later extricated.

Mrs Johnson then went with the Doctor to another incident in Broom Street, where a high explosive bomb had fallen on houses and demolished them, trapping four persons in the entry. Their services were not required at this incident so they

Mrs Amelia Johnson (Middle)

[1] *Dr Turnbull was awarded the George Medal for work in the Blitz of 1940.*

returned to the First Aid Post at Rowton House, where Mrs Johnson assisted the Doctor in rendering aid to the injured, for some hours.

This Warden went on her journeys to get assistance whilst high explosive bombs were falling and there was heavy A.A. fire, and as will be seen from the report attached. She has always shown courage and devotion to duty during the heavy air attacks, which have been made on the district in which she works. Mrs Johnson collapsed after completing her work, which lasted for many hours.

Previous Honours: Mrs Johnson had previously received a letter from Lord Dudley in connection with an incident at Birmingham Dispensary, Camp Hill, 22 October 1940.

London Gazette 18/7/1941
They – Baker, Carter and Stather -helped to rescue four men buried under debris in, Broom Street, on 9th April, 1941.

Birmingham Gazette 3/12/1941[1]
The bravery of a Birmingham woman warden in attempting to rescue eight persons who were trapped.

Mrs Amelia Johnson, of 90 Ravenhust Street, Birmingham, the warden receives the British Empire Medal. She is believed to be Britain's first woman warden to hold this medal as well as two commendations for bravery in raids. When on patrol duty Mrs Johnson found that eight people had been trapped in a demolished house. Despite falling bombs and heavy anti-air-fire she went to the incident, directed a doctor to attend and attempted to go through the cellar to effect a rescue.

Raid 9th & 10th April 1941

The Award of the George Medal (GM) to William Wilford Bennett[2]; Auxiliary Fire Service Fireman: British Empire Medal (BEM) to James Henry Meers; Auxiliary Fire Service, Fireman;
King's Commendation (KC) to Phillip Henry Bermingham; 5th Birmingham Battalion, Home Guard.

London Gazette 29/8/1941
During the raid on the 9th to the 10th April, 194, Auxiliary Firemen Meers and Bennett were on duty at the Auxiliary Fire Service Sub Station on the premises of L.H. Newton & Co Ltd. bolt, nut and screw pressing manufactures, Thimblemill Lane, Nechells.

They had already dealt with a number of incendiary bombs, which had penetrated the upper floor of the four-storey block when a High Explosive bomb pierced all four floors and exploded on the ground floor making a large hole and

---

[1] *There is a photo to Mrs Johnson as part of this article.* [2] *There are photos of William Bennett, in the Evening Despatch, 3/12/1941 with his wife and child receiving his medal from Buckingham Palace.*

exposing part of a basement.

The floors above the explosion were wrecked and set on fire and a large amount of heavy machinery fell through to the ground floor. Two men who were on the second floor at the time were killed; a third man, D Murphy, who was working an operating machine, was blown by the blast through that floor and lodged across an exposed girder, where he was in grave danger of being burnt to death. He did, in fact, receive extensive burns to the face, arms and body. Meers and Bennett, although badly shaken by the explosion, heard Murphy's cries for help and entered the burning portion of the works and in an endeavour to effect a rescue.

Auxiliary Fireman Bennett

Meers tried to make his way up the staircase, but this had collapsed under the weight of falling masonry. Bennett in the meantime had located Murphy. In his first attempt to reach him he was beaten back by the flames. He finally succeeded in

L. H. Newton & Co. Ltd after the bombing of the 9th & 10th April

reaching from the staircase, joined him and they then together succeeded in bringing the injured man to safety.

The fire spread rapidly and involved the whole work making it necessary to evacuate a large basement shelter housing 400 employees, several of whom had been injured and were receiving treatment in the first-aid department.

Despite the intense heat and dense smoke, Meers and Bennett helped to remove these persons and later, hearing cries for help from the basement which had become charged with smoke, made another entry to guide out two men who were in difficulties. They then rejoined their Auxiliary Fire Service colleagues and helped attack the fire.

There can be no doubt that Meers and Bennett saved the life of Murphy and throughout showed the highest courage and disregard of their personal safety.

London Gazette 13/1/1941

This NCO, Phillip Henry Bermingham, showed great courage and devotion to duty on the night of 9th to the 10th April, 1941. During an enemy air attack the factory, which he was guarding, was hit by high explosive bombs and caught fire. Although the raid was still in progress he played a prominent part in the evacuation of 400 workpeople from the building. In spite of the fact that the building was by this time ablaze and beginning to collapse, he broke his way through to the armoury and recovered and brought to safety all the arms and ammunition of his Home Guard unit.

Raid 9th to 10th April 1941

The award of the George Medal (GM): Thomas Montague William Henwood; Police Constable E.157

London Gazette 20/6/1941[1]

During an air raid on the 9th to the 10th April 1941, Henwood, was responsible, after mustering fire watchers to form a chain, in preventing the spread of fire. Also he went to a wrecked house where two persons were trapped. He began to move the debris and after working for about half an hour, he succeeded in releasing a woman. During this time high explosive bombs fell nearby and part of the wall of another house collapsed close to him. Despite this, he continued his efforts and rescued another casualty. Owing to the dangerous condition of the surrounding buildings, Police Constable Henwood allowed no one to work with him and it was by his efforts alone that the two persons were released.

Report from newspaper, not identified.

Gallant Policeman: Rescues Two Women From Sparkhill Fire.

Although he had dislocated his collar-bone, a Birmingham Policeman refused to

---

[1] *Henwood's George Medal is in the keeping of the Police Museum.*

Police Constables Henwood and Jackson[1]

give up his rescue efforts at a Sparkhill fire yesterday, and forcing his way into a burning house lowered two women from a bed room window before making his escape down a rope then collapsed.

The fire was in the living room of 3 Tiverton Terrace, Poplar Road, Sparkhill, and the only two occupants of the house – Mrs Clara Davis and her daughter Alice – were unable to leave the bed room through the dense volumes of smoke.

Police Constable Henwood, who, with Sergeant Stewart was near the house on his beat, heard the women's screams, and while a hunt was being made for a ladder, made an attempt to reach the women.

Going upstairs, he fell and dislocated his collar-bone, but succeeded in reaching the women and lowering them to safety. After making his own escape he had to be taken to the General Hospital, but was later discharged.[2]

---

[1] *Photo of Henwood receiving his George Medal from Buckingham Palace, with PC Jackson.*
[2] *Front cover image shows Henwood meeting Prime Minister Winston Churchill.*

Raid 9th to 10th April 1941

The Award of the British Empire Medal (BEM): William Gay, Motorman, Birmingham City Transport; Clifford Saywell, Mechanic, Birmingham City Transport; Harold Titchen, Mechanic, Birmingham City Transport[1]; Tom Jones, Warden, Civil Defence.

London Gazette 2/1/1942

A number of men and women were in the Mess Room, having come from the shelter during a lull, when it was struck by high explosive bombs. The roof collapsed and some were buried under debris. The building caught fire, but despite this W. Titchen, C. Saywell and W. Gay and a member of the Voluntary Rescue Squad, Mr T. Jones repeatedly entered the Mess Room and brought out the injured. They then found that a Conductor and a Conductress, although trapped under the debris, were still alive. At this time fire was enveloping the Mess Room and the position had become so serious that Saywell's clothing caught fire. The men were only able to continue their work by pouring water over each other. They were able to release the two employees, the air raid continuing throughout the whole of the operation.

Report of the Transport Committee 22nd April 1941

At the Miller Street Depot a number of men and women were in the Mess room having come from the Shelter during a lull, it is stated, to warm themselves, when it was struck by a high explosive bomb. The roof collapsed and some were buried under debris. The building caught fire, but despite this, Mechanic W. Titchen, Mechanic C Saywell and Motorman Gay No. 1273 and a member of the Voluntary

Titchen, Saywell and Gay

---

[1] *There is a photograph of Gay, Saywell and Titchen in the Birmingham Gazette, 100t January 1942, above a story entitled "Drenched With Water to Defy Blaze."*

Rescue Squad, Mr T. Jones[1] of 5 Back of 75 Frederick Place, Miller Street, repeatedly entered the Mess Room and brought out the injured. They then found that Conductor Lutwych and Conductress Kent although trapped under the debris were still alive. At this the fire was enveloping the Mess Room and the position had become so serious that Saywell's clothing caught fire. The men were only able to continue their work by pouring water over each other. They were able to release the two employees, the Air Raid continuing throughout the whole of the operation.

Raid Date Unknown

The Award of the British Empire Medal (BEM): William Hall, 1/29 Latimer Street, Foreman ARP Rescue Party; William Carlin, 8 Gordon Street, Member ARP Rescue Party; John Partridge, 6/44 Cowpeter Street, Member ARP Rescue Party; Frederick Skitt, 126 Dollman Street, Member ARP Rescue Party.

London Gazette 1/8/1941
During an air raid a building was hit by high explosive and incendiary bombs. Two men were pinned by the legs under blocks of concrete and were surrounded by flames. Hall, Carlin, Partridge and Skitt, without thought for their own safety, worked so close to the fire that the remainder of the party made a chain and threw buckets of water on them to prevent their clothes catching fire. After nearly two hours, during which time high explosive bombs and incendiaries were falling very near to the scene of the incident, the two-trapped persons were released.

Raid 10th April 1941

The Award of the British Empire Medal (BEM): Charles Ernest Rudge, Senior ARP Warden; Charles Williams Bowker, ARP Warden; Geoffrey Canning, Police Constable.

London Gazette 20/6/1941
At about 12:30am on Thursday 10th April, 1941 a high explosive bomb fell in Osborn Road, Sparkbrook demolishing houses 8, 10 and 12. Walter Morton, 34 years old, was trapped and buried in debris at number 12. Senior Warden Rudge and Warden Bowker were on duty and went to the scene. They found a Mr Hill was injured at number 14 and whilst Bowker was getting the man away Rudge ran to the Wardens Post in Stratford Road. Bowker made enquires and ascertained Morton was beneath the debris. Constable Canning arrived and the two men made a search and heard muffled cries. Rudge returned and the three men then started digging and sawing through heavy furniture, wooden joists, chairs, staircase etc. to get to the mans head. After about three-quarters of and hour they saw Morton's face, which

---

[1] *It appears the Mr T. Jones was also a recipient of the Military Medal (MM), in the First World War.*

had been covered by an overcoat, so breathing was obstructed. Morton's face was fanned and Bowker and the Constable allowed water to run down their arms on to his face, after which his condition appeared to improve. He was however trapped by the legs and Bowker and Canning continued sawing through the debris for nearly three hours until Morton was rescued. During this time slates and brickwork fell from over hanging parts of the roof and Bowker and Canning removed their steel helmets and put them over Morton's face and head to prevent him from sustaining further injury. Rudge engaged him in conversation to keep him cheerful whilst the rescue work was in progress, and after nearly three hours these men were able to get the injured man out of the debris ad send him to a first aid post. Further, whilst carrying

P.C. Canning

out their work, enemy aircraft were overhead and there were bombs, as well as shrapnel, dropping in the district.

The Wardens and the constable worked well and no doubt saved the man's life by their continued efforts to free him from the debris.

Raid 10th April 1941

The Award of the British Empire Medal (BEM): John Payne[1], Police Constable C.201; Robert Ellis Pritchard, Firewatcher.

London Gazette 1/8/1941

About 12.45am on Thursday, 10th April 1941, during a heavy air attack two high explosive bombs dropped in Edward Street and Scotland Street, Ladywood, very close together. The one in Edward Street did considerable damage to houses in that street, but there were no casualties. The second bomb fell in Scotland Street smashing the rear of No. 2 and burying the occupants Alfred Hood and his wife Alice. The bomb also demolished the house at the rear and seven persons, including three children, were buried in the ruins of this house.

Police Constable C.201 John Payne arrived and was informed of what had happened. He at once got busy and with valuable assistance of Mr Robert Pritchard, commenced to remove the brickwork and debris from around where the two persons were known to be buried. It was very dangerous work as not only the air attack being continued locally, and bombs falling, but the walls that were left standing adjoining

---

[1] *Payne was 26 years of age when this incident occurred and had been a police constable for four and a half years. He lived at 205, Soho Road, Handsworth, Birmingham.*

to where they were working were in immediate danger of collapse and there was a complete staircase hanging in a precarious position over their heads, which looked as if it might fall at any time. It was necessary for both Pritchard and Payne to sit in the hole with their backs to the brickwork while they worked, and this brickwork was continually slipping but by doing this they prevented it falling into the part where they believed Mr and Mrs Hood to be, but their awkward position retarded the progress of their work. Eventually a woman's arm was exposed, they worked harder than ever and then heard a mans faint voice. They uncovered more of the debris and found the man and woman practically locked together. At this time further brickwork fell and covered the lower part of the legs of both rescuers, but handicapped as they were and in constant peril from falling bombs and debris they worked on and at about 3.30am were able to remove Alfred Hood from the debris, and was taken to hospital [where he has made a good recovery]. Mrs Hood was afterwards removed but unfortunately was found to be dead.

Several other persons rendered intermittent assistance in the rescue, but the bulk of the work fell on Payne and Pritchard[1].

After the above rescue had been completed, PC Payne and Mr Pritchard went to the ruins of the other houses, that people were buried in the cellar. It was impossible to reach them from the ordinary cellar entrance as this was completely blocked up with tons of debris, but the rescue squad which was present, made every effort to do so. Payne then went into the cellar next door and with the valuable assistance form George Thomas Brett [from 64 Edward St] and Edward Charles Willard [from 74 The Parade] and again accompanied by Pritchard, he commenced to tunnel through the wall of this cellar in an effort to reach the buried people [they heard a child's voice asking for his daddy, and this caused them to work faster]. They worked for several hours until relieved by the Rescue Squad.

Raid 10th April 1941

The Award of the British Empire Medal (BEM): Charles Frederick Ward, Police Sergeant.

London Gazette 20/6/1941

On Wednesday to Thursday the 9th and 10th April 1941, a severe air attack was made on the centre of the city in the course of which a stick of five bombs was dropped, the high explosive bombs damaged the Police Headquarters, Coroner's Court etc. in Steel house Lane. In Weaman Street, which is off Steelhouse Lane, one bomb destroyed the British Hub Company, and another penetrated the factory of Messrs Webley & Scott, at about 1am; some ten feet from the observation post where Cpl Albert Harry Dunn of the Home Guard and his men were on duty.

Dunn immediately began a search and eventually located it. The bomb, a 550 lb.

---

[1] *Pritchard was 33 years of age when he was involved in the rescue, he was a self employed window cleaner by trade and lived at 113, Westminster Rd, Handsworth, Birmingham.*

was a delayed action high explosive type which had penetrated through two floors and came to rest in a ground floor workshop. The works were on vital war production and were working night shifts, but the personnel were in shelters in the factory at the time. Dunn, the Home Guard and Works Police escorted the all to safe shelters nearby.

Cpl Dunn[1] and Volunteer White then went to the police station and reported the presence of the bomb. At 2:30am Police Sergeant Charles F. Ward arrive and assisted by Cpl Dunn, L/Cpl Causier and Fire Officer Dibble who held the torches Ward found that the top of the bomb was loose, by using tools found nearby, he took out the fuse (12" x 2") and put it in a bucket of water. The bomb was removed by the Bomb Disposal Company at 5pm and the employees were able to resume work at 8:30am.

Interview with Sergeant Ward, Birmingham Evening Mail, 5/2/1979
His action won him the British Empire Medal; but bravery was almost commonplace on that awful night when much of the heart of Birmingham was destroyed and the Men in Blue were in he thick of it; certainly at "A" Division headquarters Steelhouse Lane. But the "All Clear" had sounded and when Sergeant Ward got back from what should have been his last incident of the night; then came news of an unexploded bomb in the middle of Loveday Street.

"I got back to find the Chief with a message in his hand saying, 'there's a ticklish one here. It is Webley & Scotts[2] and you know it is a Category 1 factory' (which meant it had police protection at all times). He warned me to be careful and suggested the railway authorities should be told as a big explosion there would affect Snow Hill station.

We got down to Slaney Street – which disappeared with the creation of Colmore Circus. Outside the works the police officer simply pointed and said: 'it's in there.' A sergeant in the factory Home Guard let me in, saying, 'there's a real beauty down in the basement'. However, we went up first to check where it had come through. There was not only a beautiful hole in the roof, but we could follow the bomb's track straight down through four floors, and amazingly right through an open dust bin and it was lying in the basement among the cases of automatic guns. It was a big one, about six-foot at least. The great yellow fins with 'screamers' were still on but the top filler cap had been dislodged and I got my hand in, scooping out the explosive like soft cheese to reach the fuse from inside.

Fortunately the fuse was loose, but once I'd got it out I didn't really know what the hell to do with it. Here we were the Home Guard sergeant still watching from around a corner, in a works of vital importance. And of course, the fuse itself could be damaging – certainly it could kill a man. Anyhow I put it in a bucket of water, covered it all with sandbags and we all beat a hasty retreat.

When I got back to Steelhouse Lane I sent a report 'UXB Webley & Scott confirmed. Fuse removed, incident closed'.

---

[1] *Cpl. Albert Harry Dunn and L/Cpl Causier were awarded certificates for gallantry.*
[2] *The Webley & Scott factory was on the site of the present Post and Mail building.*

Raid 10th April 1941

The Award of the British Empire Medal (BEM); Charles Hartley Forster, Aircraft Foreman, 2 Lloyd Street, Small Heath; Joseph Jones, Motor Driver, 100 Golden Hillock Road; Alan Ernest Underwood, Police Constable E.2000. King's Commendation (KC); Edwin Gilbert Robberds, ARP Warden, 54 Golden Hillock Road.

London Gazette 25/7/1941

At about 12.30am on Thursday, 10th April 1941 a high explosive bomb fell in Golden Hillock Road partially demolishing houses number 43, 45 and 47 and igniting a gas main. Jones went to the scene and first moved a motor car, which was near to the fire. Forster went to several houses nearby and made sure that no one was trapped. They then went to No.47 and found someone was buried in the debris. Jones and Forster commenced to move the debris. Some tools were obtained and Forster started to saw through a door and other timber, and after some time a man was partially uncovered. It was then found that a second man was also buried, and Forster and Jones worked hard to clear the debris away from him[1].

Police Constable Underwood then arrived on the scene, and the three of them worked under most difficult conditions in as endeavour to get the buried men out. Warden Robberds went to the scene and found that rescue work was in progress at No.47 PC Underwood, Joseph Jones and Charles Forster were at work and owing to the restricted space, Robberds was unable to assist at first. Later on, however, he relieved the rescuers for short periods and worked under difficult and dangerous conditions. The roof of the house was leaning, and continually slipping. It was necessary at the time to stop work in order to prop the roof up, and up to about 2.30am bombs were falling in the neighbourhood.

The two buried men were extracted at 6.30am and about one hour after they had been released the roof collapsed.

Raid 10th April 1941

The Award of the George Medal (GM); Charles Arthur Freeman, ARP Warden.

London Gazette 13/6/1941

At 01.15 hours, Thursday, 10th April, 194, when heavy air raid was in progress, a high explosive bomb of very heavy calibre fell in Lawden Road, Small Heath, in front of dwelling houses 38 to 43, which houses were completely demolished, eight persons being trapped beneath the debris. Sewers, gas mains and electric cables were severed and a large crater was made in the roadway. Warden Freeman was on

---

[1] *The men rescued were Robert Orr and Thomas Banister.*

patrol in the vicinity, made a survey and went to the Wardens Post to report, returning immediately to the incident, and was joined by his Group Warden and others. Trapped persons were heard groaning, and one seriously injured casualty was rescued and sent to Hospital. Warden Freeman tunnelled beneath the debris at the edge of the crater and entered the hole, which he had made with his hands. He handed out some of the debris and worked until about 5am when he recovered the body of another Warden. Twenty minutes later he recovered another body. He continued working until 6.30am when the Rescue Squad arrived.

During the time Freeman was working in the hole, debris was overhanging and there was a strong escape of gas. High explosive bombs and shrapnel from Anti-Aircraft fire were dropping in the vicinity,

Mr. C. A. Freeman

Lawden Road after the raid of 10th April

and his position was extremely dangerous. A slight fire also broke out near to where he was engaged in rescue operations.

Warden Freeman showed courage of a high order, and worked unceasingly in a determined effort to rescue the trapped people. His action is worthy of recognition.

Later in the day a man, severely injured, was rescued and the bodies of four other persons were recovered.

Evening Mail 5/2/1979

"I wouldn't talk about it then – and I don't really want to talk about it now" says Mr Charles Arthur Freeman GM. It was the night the Germans blasted Brum with 190,000 kilograms of bombs – the night of April 9th to 10th 1941; when Senior Air Raid Warden Freeman won the George Medal. For much of that dreadful raid he tunnelled among the debris of a row of demolished houses in Lawden Road. Small Heath, to succour for survivors and bring out the dead. Charles Freeman is only one of many who performed brave deeds that night and – as he stresses – on many another night. Not all of them lived. Not all of them were honoured.

Today, 37 year on, Mr Freeman and his wife live the quiet life of pensioners in an unassuming house in Harborne. "We are not grumblers" he says, "and we manage to enjoy life without any luxuries. I enjoy my few cigarettes – but I can't remember when we last went out to a show. I have an allotment which I can still work – given better weather – despite a couple of heart attacks."

He talks with pride of the way people were in those wartime days – and nights. He doesn't think it noteworthy to have done nights of duty as a Senior Warden near their home and then never missed a day from work in a local munitions factory. "At one stage we spent five months without ever taking our clothes off", he says. "But everyone performed what now seems miracles."

Of the Blitz he says that the area of Small Heath where they lived was a constant target for the German bombers. "Even when they'd been having a go somewhere close it always seemed they kept a couple for us on the way back", he said. "It wasn't surprising as there are two main rail lines with a bottom track to the marshalling yards, a canal, bridges carrying vital lines of communication and factories all around."

He believes the stick of bombs that destroyed the houses in Lawden Road were aimed at the two bridges between were they were situated. "Two minutes later and I would have gone with them," said Mr Freeman. "That's how far I was away – they fell as I was walking along Boulton Road to contact the warden in charge of the sector. "The lot came down and there was nothing but dust and smoke. I tore back to report it but the post warden at Oakley Road said the phones were out and just shrugged his shoulders. I ran back: there were incendiaries everywhere. The dust was settling and the only thing to do was to start shifting bricks … the third body I found was that of the warden …

Mr Freeman still does not know how many died in that one incident – "about nine I think" – or how many were injured. Even when help came his problems were not over. "It was chaos really – people just waded in, it was difficult to organise. At one point I thought we would all be buried under the walls I could see swaying". It was later that year that he went to Buckingham Palace to receive his medal from King George VI with his wife and two young daughters – "It was our greatest day". What of today? "Well we could certainly do with some of the spirit the people showed in those days – but we shall never see the like of it again".

Raid 10th April 1941

The Award of the King's Commendation (KC); Dr Alexander Henday MacKie, M.D. 73 years old, Washwood Heath Road; Alfred Smith, ARP Section Warden, 164 Northleigh Road, Ward End; William Pritchard, Temp Sergeant D. 114, 90 Hancock Road, Alum Rock; Alfred Edwin John Smith, Acetylene Welder, aged 14 years, Ward End Road; Charles Marson, ARP Section Warden, 53 Drews Lane, Ward End; James Harper, Barman, 139 Northleigh Road, Ward End.

London Gazette 25/7/1941
During an air raid on 10th April 1941 a high explosive bomb demolished two houses and several persons were buried in the debris. The above men were concerned in the rescue of a man buried under debris and pinned down by a piano. Dr MacKie walked half a mile to the scene, while bombs were falling and gave the man morphia.

Birmingham Gazette 26/7/1941
Air raid, Ward End Road, on the 10th April 1941, a high explosive bomb demolished two houses and several persons were buried in debris. (This is off Drews Lane, Washwood Heath)

Raid 10th April 1941

The Award of the British Empire Medal (BEM); John Francis Clancey, Auxiliary Fireman.

London Gazette 22/8/1941
During the air raid on Birmingham on the night of Thursday, the 10th April, 1941, premises at Messrs. Postans, Morley Bros. & Birthles Ltd. Paint, Varnish and Oil Manufactures in Trevor Street, Birmingham, at which an Auxiliary Fire Service works sub-station had been established were struck by incendiary bombs.

The north-east block of the factory was soon well alight and the wind rapidly drove the flames towards the major portion of the building in Trevor Street.

Whilst the fire was being attacked a terrific explosion occurred in the burning part of the building when a bomb was dropped amongst the varnish tanks igniting some 5,000 gallons of varnish. The man on the first branch had been obliged to withdraw but Auxiliary Clancey without hesitation went to the edge of the fire and directed the jet. His Station Officer told him to try and check the spread to the fire towards him whilst he (the Officer) went to arrange for more assistance jets to be brought. When the Officer turned to Clancey he found that he had not only succeeded in checking the spread of the flames but had actually driven the fire back. There was imminent danger of an explosion occurring in the adjoining shop where 3 cwts of nitro-cellulose plastic was stored. Clancey knew this as the AFS men employed by

Auxiliary Fireman Clancey

the firm had reported the fact, and had it not been for his courageous stand the fire would no doubt have spread very rapidly and created a serious situation.

Throughout this action large numbers of high explosive bombs were dropped in the area and Clancey had also been advised of delayed action bombs near the premises.

Raid 10th April 1941

The Award of the British Empire Medal (BEM); John Henry Morson, ARP Warden; David Watson, Police Reserve Constable E 409[1]

London Gazette 25/7/1941
At about 00.45 hours on Thursday the 10th April 1941, First Police Reserve E.409 Watson was on duty in Grange Road, Small Heath, during an intense enemy air raid, when a high explosive bomb fell and hit a number of houses in Bertram Road, No 5, 7, 9, 11 and 13 were demolished. In company with Air Raid Warden John Morson of 5 Wyndcliffe Road, Small Heath, he went to the scene and on examining the debris heard people groaning underneath the wreckage. He sent a message by messenger for a rescue party, the telephones in the locality being out of order, and together with Morson commenced to search the wreckage. He was assisted for a time by people in the neighbourhood but these gave up the task after a short time and he and Warden Morson continued with the work above, receiving some direction from George Henry Rainsford, husband of one of the buried women.

They carried on with the search for about one and a half hours during which time

---
[1] *There is a picture of PC Watson and a short account of the incident in the Birmingham Gazette 26/7/1941, p.3.*

high explosive bombs were falling in the vicinity and flares from enemy aircraft were illuminating the scene. After removing a large quantity to debris they eventually saw a woman's hand thrust into the open. They continued to remove the surrounding debris and a few minutes afterwards succeeded in dragging one of the women Elizabeth May Rainsford, aged 25, who had been sheltering under the staircase and was trapped when the house collapsed into the open. After handing her to people, standing near they continued and after a short time released her mother Elizabeth Rainsford from the same place. Both women were without serious injury and were attended to by neighbours. After releasing the two women, Watson and Warden Morson continued the search as it was known that two other persons were in the house, but gave up, upon the arrival of a rescue squad at about 0230 hours.

At 0430 hours, the dead bodies of Mr and Mrs Charles Rainsford (Junior) 11 Bertram Road were recovered from the debris.

It was due to the efforts of Constable Watson and Warden Morson that the women were rescued from the wreckage of the houses alive. The district in which the incident took place was subjected to a particularly vicious attack during the time that the rescue was being carried out. There being a delayed action bomb within about 30 yards of the scene and another high explosive bomb fell a few yards in Baker Street about 20 yards away which caused several fatal casualties and widespread damage to property.

Raid 11th April 1941

The Award of the British Empire Medal (BEM); Joseph Thomas Flavell[1], Police Sergeant C20; King's Commendation (KC); Robert Duck, Police Constable C55.

London Gazette 1/8/1941

At about 12.45am, on Friday 11th April, 1941, during an enemy air attack a number of incendiary bombs dropped in the streets and on premises in the vicinity of Hockley Brook, one of these bombs falling on the roof of the promises of Messrs Shakeshafts, wholesale and retail grocers, 89 Hockley Hill. A fire was started between the rafters and roof and the premises very quickly became full of thick, choking smoke, owing to the nature of the articles on fire. Mr Shakeshaft in addition to two members of a local sector Fire Party, entered the premises, but two of them returned to the street immediately, being partly overcome by the dense smoke. One of these Henry Evans informed his nephew Albert Bennett who took a bucket of water and forced his way upstairs, but after reaching the first floor was compelled to return to the open air. Meanwhile Mr Shakeshaft himself had reached the second floor and attempted to deal with the burning bomb and building, but he also was compelled to leave after a short time.

---

[1] *Flavell was also involved with another incident on August 26th 1940, where he aided by PC Bill Price. There is a photo and account of PC's Payne and Flavell in the, Birmingham Gazette,2/81/1941.*

The two officers, Flavell and Duck entered the premises before Mr Shakeshaft left and they attempted to reach the bomb. Flavell smashed a hole in the plaster with his truncheon and Duck enlarged the hole with an axe and they then played on the flames with a jet from a stirrup pump, which was being fed by various civilians. Conditions were extremely bad and it was almost impossible to breathe in this room owing to the smoke. Both officers used handkerchiefs round their mouths, which helped matters somewhat. Duck obtained another pump and getting a little higher was able to get nearer the flames but his position was extremely hazardous, and as flames were reaching wood and various articles underneath his feet, he was compelled to leave this position, but the results of their efforts was that the fire was being kept under control, although goods in this room were burned and several doors badly scorched.

Constable Duck suddenly collapsed owing to the smoke in his lungs and Sergeant Flavell was compelled to leave his fire fighting and go to Ducks assistance. Owing to the thick smoke it was difficult and almost impossible for the Sergeant to find his whereabouts and the room and the stairs were littered with goods and empty cases. In addition to this, the stairs are winding and steep, the premises being very old and even under favourable conditions in daylight it is difficult to negotiate. Constable Duck is a very heavy man, over fourteen stone in weight yet Sergeant Flavell carried him down two flights of stairs past all kinds of obstructions, which left scarcely room to pass in the smoke laden atmosphere and the pitch dark. It was necessary to go through two rooms in addition to going down stairs and these rooms were full of goods, but by Herculean efforts the Sergeant succeeded in reaching the street where he also collapsed. They recovered, but declined to go to hospital and remained on duty. Flavell then went to an incident where five persons were killed and two injured, and he assisted in getting out one of the injured men from the debris. He then helped an Inspector bring an explosive device to the Police Station, and continued his duties until 6am.

Sergeant Flavell and constable Duck acted in a most commendable manner and showed courage and devotion to duty throughout the night.

Raid 10th to 11th April 1941

The Award of the British Empire Medal (BEM): Frederick William Lloyd, Driver Birmingham City Transport; Sidney Clifford Miller, Driver Birmingham City Transport.[1]

London Gazette 15/8/1941
During an air raid incendiary bombs fell on omnibuses parked on Garrison Lane recreation ground. One of the buses was set on fire. Lloyd got into the cabin of the burning bus whilst Miller moved the machine in front. Lloyd drove his bus out of

---

[1] *There is a photograph of both Lloyd and Miller in the, Birmingham Gazette, 16/8/1941, p.3.*

the park, but fire spread so rapidly that on reaching the road the vehicle burned out despite the efforts of the fire brigade. These men performed an outstanding service in a most courageous manner, disregarding the great danger , valuable rolling stock was saved from destruction. Miller had already driven a burning bus out of the park in the air raid of the 9th to the 10th of April 1941[1].

Raid 11th April 1941

The Award of the British Empire Medal (BEM); John Gandy, ARP Warden; Robert Maurice Strangward, ARP Warden; Frederick Butler Miles, Police Constable.

London Gazette 19/9/1941

At about 1.30am on Friday 11th April 1941, during an air attack on the City, a high explosive bomb was dropped in City Road; partly demolishing houses No 128 and 130.

Warden Strangward, accompanied by PC Miles and Warden Gandy arrived at the scene a few minutes after the bomb had fallen and ascertained that two persons, Mr and Mrs Steele had been sleeping in a room on the first floor at the rear of No 130 City Road when the bomb dropped.

Owing to the condition of the buildings, to reach the first floor it was necessary to climb up the wall of No 128, the brickwork of which was crumbling and precarious. Whilst climbing this wall Warden Strangward sustained an injury to his right knee and PC Miles fell and was in danger of becoming buried himself, but all three men finally reached the room were the two persons were buried under three or four feet of masonry and debris. They commenced to remove this debris, and after removing a large quantity they uncovered Mrs Steele, who was injured though conscious. Warden Strangward carried her to the ground floor, which to reach it , it was necessary to walk along a single wall, which was in a precarious condition, before the staircase was gained.

PC Miles and Warden Gandy continued to remove further debris and finally rescued Mr Steel, who was then carried by PC Miles, assisted by Warden Gandy, to the ground floor.

During the whole of the time the rescue work was going on the building was shaking and in danger of further collapse. The air raid continued, flares being dropped in the neighbourhood.

---

[1] *Both Lloyd and Miller were drivers from the Liverpool Street Garage.*

Raid 1941

The Award of the King's Commendation (KC); Percy Lionel Edward Shurmer[1], Member Volunteer Sector Fire Party; Raymond Williams, Member Volunteer Sector Fire Party.

London Gazette 20/6/1941

During an air raid bombs demolished some property trapping five persons in a cellar. They saw that the front of the premises was in a dangerous condition and heard shouting from beneath the debris. After considerable work in removing the debris they found that the floor had caved in and the entrance to the cellar was blocked. They cut a hole in the floor and rescued two others and recovered the body of the fifth.

Percy Shurmer

Percy Shurmer

Percy Shurmer was born in Cheltenham, in 1888. He had served in the 48th Division in the First World War, but was demobilised in 1917 after being wounded and gassed. He became a Labour Co-operative councillor for St Martin's ward, in Birmingham, in 1921, and was briefly imprisoned after the General Strike of 1926 for "causing disaffection". He was elected an Alderman in 1934 and in 1945 he became the Labour MP for Sparkbrook, a seat that he held until his death in 1959.

Date Unknown

The Award of the King's Commendation (KC); Mrs Annie Elizabeth Smith, Member of the British Red Cross Society.

London Gazette 20/21/1942

Mrs Smith, member of the "Birmingham 40" Detachment, The British Red Cross Society, was on night duty in Tyburn Road, Erdington during an air raid. It was a dark night and she tripped over a body lying in the road. She found it was a young man and that one leg of his trousers was soaked with blood. She realised that this was coming from his main artery, and at once pressed hard on the femoral artery and did not let go until help arrived.

---

[1] There is a photograph of Percy Shurmer in the, *Birmingham Gazette, 21/6/1941.*

Raid 17th May 1941

The Award of the British Empire Medal (BEM); Evan James Davies, Probationary Police Constable; Jasper Leslie Fowler, Police Constable.

London Gazette 22/8/1941

At 1.45am on 17th May 1941 a high explosive bomb fell in Scholefield St, Nechells, demolishing dwelling houses 155 to 164 and several casualties resulted. PC D208 Fowler and PPC D287 Davies went to the scene and Fowler took charge, and they were told of several people trapped. They heard screams coming from beneath debris at No 155 and climbing over the debris they found three women in the cellar (Mrs Jennie Louisa Ferris and her two companions Miss Marion Gladys Stone and Mrs Cummings both of 1/179 Scholefield St). The constables removed debris with their hands, and were able to lift the women up through the floor of the kitchen, which had collapsed into the cellar. The women were suffering from shock.

One of the women (Mrs Ferris) told the constables that her husband with two other men had been standing in the entry adjoining the demolished houses when the bomb fell. They commenced to search the debris and heard voices, so got a pick and shovel and worked alternately to move sufficient debris to reach the entry door, which had been blown off and was wedged on either side. PC Fowler, as above, forced up the door and whilst Constable Davies supported it he crawled into the debris and was able to drag out the three trapped men. They were all suffering from shock, cuts and bruises and were taken to Hospital. During this time part of the damaged buildings collapsed about the constables.

They then searched in other damaged and dangerous property, cellars etc and at a back house heard moans. They told the Rescue Squad and with them worked until two people were rescued, and the body of another person was got out. The constables worked until 4.30am. The raid continued, bombs were dropped in the district, and there was anti-aircraft fire. The PC's actions are worthy of recognition.

Raid 28th July 1942

The Award of the British Empire Medal (BEM); John McCormack, Police Constable C97; The Award of the King's Commendation (KC); Albert Hill, War Reserve Constable C712.

London Gazette 25/9/1942

At about 2.45am on Tuesday 28th July, 1942, during an enemy air attack, a number of incendiary bombs fell in the neighbourhood of Great Hampton Street and Hockley Street. With sandbags and by means of stamping on them PC

McCormack, with assistance, put them all out. He was informed that a bomb had started a fire in the storeroom over Barclays Bank, Great Hampton Street. He could not get in, but found that caretaker in an entry, badly frightened. He took him with him, opened the premises, found the fire which had ignited a number of boxes, and with a stirrup pump extinguished the fire. He then returned to Kenyon Street and later attended the fire at the Wandsworth Electrical Co. Kenyon Street. He suggested borrowing a fire pump from Messrs. Edmonds, Constitution Hill, which he fetched himself.

PC McCormack took a jet through a house, 25 Mary Street, and in this way reached the rear of the burning premises, which were then a mass of flames, and the outer walls collapsing. He climbed a shaky ladder placed against an old wooden building, and from there played on the fire and prevented it from spreading to adjoining factories and workshops. He was assisted by Police War Reserve Constable C712, Albert Hill, who was injured. Their position at all times was hazardous, as not only was there a likelihood of the outer walls of the burning building – a four storey one – falling on them; but also the possibility of the fire spreading to the premises of Messrs. Antey and Wilsons, next door, where a quantity of varnish and lacquer is stored. The work of this officer, together with the valuable assistance rendered by other police officers, undoubtedly prevented the fire spreading to the above premises and other workshops and factories in the immediate neighbourhood.

Raid 28th July 1942

The Award of the George Medal (GM); Harold Etherington Wood[1], Police Sergeant.

The Award of the British Empire Medal (BEM); Ernest Callaghan, Police Constable; James Hughes, Mill-Wright.

London Gazette 25/9/1942
Tuesday, 28th July, 1942, at 2.15am a heavy high explosive fell on the factory of Gabriels Ltd. Coleshill Street, completely destroying it and starting two fires in the debris. Sergeant Wood went there at once and learned that about six people were trapped in an underground shelter at the works. There was a leakage of water into this shelter and the building was in danger of further collapse.

The Sergeant obtained assistance to extinguish the fires whilst he and Police Constable Callaghan endeavoured to free the trapped persons. One body was recovered from the debris and two other persons were rescued after the front wall of the factory had been broken down. A man unconscious and seriously injured was also found. During the rescue work they were joined by James Hughes, who

---

[1] *H.E. Wood had previously been awarded the, British Empire Medal (BEM), for meritorious service during air raids, in 1941.*

also rendered assistance. At 3am Fire Brigade and Rescue Squads arrived. The factory was four storeys high, each floor carrying heavy machinery, some of which, together with steel framework, was hanging in dangerous positions. During their work enemy planes were overhead and another high explosive bomb fell in the vicinity.

These three men acted in a most courageous manner without thought for their own safety. By their prompt action and determined efforts, the lives of three persons were saved[1].

P.C. Ernest Callaghan

Raid 30th July 1942

St Andrews Junction Box Near Duddeston.
The Award of the George Medal (GM): Archibald Cook, Engine Driver; George Herbert Simkiss, Fireman, London Midland & Scottish Railway.

The Award of the British Empire Medal (BEM): Richard Edward Barratt, Kitchen Porter and Home Guard; George Carter, Civil Defence Warden; William Eric Deakin, Machinist; Henry Jacob Harrison, Length Ganger LM&S Railway.

The Award of the King's Commendation (KC): Percy Edward Jones, Goods Guard LM&S Railway; James Clarke Marshall, Temp Goods Guard LM&S Railway; William Alfred Nicholls, Signalman LM&S Railway; James Reynolds, Goods Guard LM&S Railway.

London Gazette 18/12/1942
At about 1.45am Thursday, 30th July 1942 an air raid took place while a freight train, with Driver Archibald Cook, Fireman George H Simkiss and Guard James Reynolds onboard arrived in the goods yard with a load of TNT in 27 wagons and 23 other wagons. Proceeding from Bordesley Junction towards Lawley Street sidings on a journey form Gloucester to Crewe, and shortly after passing Coventry Road Bridge two wagons were struck by incendiary bombs. Fires were caused in these wagons, which were loaded with TNT in boxes of about 50lb per box. The fires were noticed by the driver on the signal at St Andrews signal box, being found to be against the train. The guard, obeying instructions left the train to inform the signal box at

---

[1] *There is a photograph of PC Callaghan and Sergeant Wood in the Birmingham Gazette, 26/9/1942.*

Bordesley Junction to inform trains arriving from that direction. The fireman informed the signal box at St Andrews for the same purpose in advising trains from the other direction. The driver, fireman and guard, assisted by the signalmen, then commenced to uncouple the blazing trucks from the main portion of the train.

Civil Defence Warden Carter arrived on the scene almost at once, also the youths W A Deakin and R E Barratt and although they were warned of the contents of the wagon and understood the danger they remained and rendered every possible assistance. They extinguished fires on the embankment which were caused by fragments thrown from the burning trucks. Carter climbed on to the trucks and did all possible until the arrival of the firemen. It was decided to endeavour to save some of the contents and the seal of one of the vans was

Harrison, Cook and Simkiss

broken. Carter and Deakin helped to pull open the door. As it opened, flames and smoke were emitted from the interior of the trucks and Carter sustained burns to the face and eyes. Deakin and Barratt also sustained slight burns to the eyes and all three required treatment at a first aid post. All present helped in removing boxes of burning TNT from the vans.

The works fire service from the New Hudson Works, Garrison Lane arrived and did all they could to hold the fires in check until the arrival of the regular National Fire Service units under D O Peters, Bordesley Green and Section Leader Gregory, Station 2.Y.

All the members of the services assisted in removing boxes of burning TNT from the vans on the fire being sufficiently controlled to enable damping down to take place. During this time the air raid continued and there was heavy anti-aircraft barrage.

From: Heroes of Road and Rail, By George C Curnock[1]

Driver Archibald Cook, with a train-load of munitions behind him, 600 tons of high explosives packed in 50 freight vans, was making all the speed he could to reach an ordnance depot during the night, when he found the signal outside a large town against him. Already he had watched the fall of incendiaries and the bursting of AA shells.

---

[1] *This is taken from George C Curnock Heroes of Road and Rail, (London, Simpkin Marshall) There is also a photograph of Harrison, Cook and Simkiss, in this publication.*

George Simkiss, his fireman, climbed down from the footplate and was halfway to the signal box to find out why the train had been stopped, when Cook called him back.

"The so-and-so's have fired the train" bellowed the driver. One van was already alight. Both men did their best to put out the fire. It was too much for them. They did the next best thing. Uncoupling this van, Cook sent Simkiss to look for help, and then pulled the front part of the train clear of it with all the steam he could crowd on.

"Then I ran back" he says. "The blighters had got us again. Simkiss uncoupled once more, and I pulled another section to safety." All this time the raiders were busy overhead and Cook had already had an ankle injured by a shell splinter while running up and down the track.

While this was going on and one van already bursting with small explosions, Ganger Henry Harrison arrived with three Home Defence workers, two only 17 years old. Cook's advice to the youths was: "Clear out. This is our job. There's enough here to blow you as high as a plane".

The three young defenders stayed and helped to open a burning van. Flames burned their faces. Ganger Harrison told them to "get to hell out of here"; "but he might as well have asked Jerry to stop slinging down bombs. They carried on as calmly as if they were cleaning the kitchen table". So he left them to help the National Fire Service, now at the scene of action, and turned to the task of heaving heavy boxes of explosive out of another wagon on the line, and then to clearing the line after the danger was passed, despite burned hands and soaked clothes.

29th November 1942

Pheasey Farm Grenade Range
The Award of the King's Commendation (KC): G H Rowe, Sergeant 12th Birmingham (Public Utilities) Battalion. Home Guard.

London Gazette 11/3/1943
Sergeant Rowe was assisting in the supervision of a live grenade throwing practice by squad under instruction at Pheasey Farm Grenade Range, Birmingham, on 29th November 1942.

One man failed to clear the top of the parapet with his throw and the grenade rolled back into the bay. He attempted to pick it up again but Sergeant Rowe, realising the danger of its immediate detonation, pushed the man away and literally carried him away from the throwing bay to safety.

Later a second man dropped his grenade after extracting the pin. In a moment of panic he attempted to climb out of the bay. Again Sergeant Rowe saved the situation by forcing the man away, pushing him to the ground and flinging himself on top of him. On this occasion a fragment of the bursting grenade cut into Sergeant Rowe's greatcoat.[1]

Birmingham Gazette 23rd March 1943
The heroism of a Birmingham Home Guard Sergeant was marked by a pleasing ceremony at Liverpool Street bus garage last night.

Sergeant Rowe

During a concert at the garage, Major General G.G. Waterhouse presented a citation on behalf of the King to Sergeant G Rowe, a popular Selly Oak bus driver, who saved two Home Guard Privates during a demonstration of live grenade throwing, at a local range on November Sunday last year.

On the first occasion a Private dropped a live grenade in the throwing bay and became stupefied by the mishap. Sergeant Rowe "jumped to it". Without hesitation he threw the man to one side and covered him with his own body as the grenade exploded. The only injuries were to the Sergeants uniform.

Half an hour later there was a similar incident, when a grenade hit the parapet and rolled back into the throwing bay, this time the Private rushed to climb out of the bay, but Rowe caught hold of him, dropped on top of him to shield him and received the only injuries inflicted – luckily no more than scratches from flying shrapnel.[2]

---

[1] *The citation was presented to Sergeant Rowe at Liverpool Street bus garage on 22th March, 1943 by Major General G.G. Waterhouse on behalf of the King. Sergeant Rowe also received the British Empire Medal in the Birthday Honours List and appears in the London Gazette of 8/6/1944.*
[2] *There is a photograph of Sergeant G.H. Rowe in the history of Birmingham Home Guard.*

Appendix One

The award of King's Commendation for which no date or location of incident has been traced.

Miss Georgine Nelly Adam	London Gazette 14/3/1941	ARP Warden
Leslie Joseph Arkinstall	London Gazette 21/2/1941	Auxiliary Fireman AFS
Harold Emery	London Gazette 7/3/1941	Member, Works Fir Brigade
James Henry Fitzgerald	London Gazette 17/1/1941	Works Maintenance Engineer
William Ford	London Gazette 14/3/1941	ARP Section Warden
David Gumbley		Fitters Mate
James Gumbley	London Gazette 14/3/1941	Millwright
James Edward Hayward	London Gazette 7/3/1941	Member, Works Fire Brigade
Wilfred Ketley	London Gazette 7/3/1941	Tinsmith
William James Larcombe	London Gazette 20/12/1941	Technical Advisor, Civil Defence
Robert Henry Llewellyn	London Gazette 7/3/1941	Member, Works Fire Brigade
Richard Wilfred Martin	london Gazette 24/1/1941	Chief Fireman, Works AFS
Albert Mayne	London Gazette 25/4/1941	Section Officer AFS
Albert Thomas Morgan	London Gazette 30/1/1942	Driver
Ronald Charles Phillips	London Gazette 25/9/1942	Messenger, Civil Defence
Cyril John Potter	London Gazette 21/3/1941	Deputy Head, ARP Warden
Mrs Ada Louise Rose	London Gazette 12/12/1940	ARP Warden
Harold Shepherd	London Gazette 3/1/1941	Fire Watcher, ARP
Howell Thomas	London Gazette 7/3/1941	ARP Sector Warden
Norman Whalley	London Gazette 25/9/1942	Probationary Police Officer
Hardy Whitehouse	London Gazette 24/1/1941	Commissioner, ARP Warden
Patrick Walter Wilkie	London Gazette 30/1/1942	Demolition Foreman
Mrs Irene Rachel Williams	London Gazette 25/9/1942	Staff Warden, Civil Defence
Charles Patrick Wright	London Gazette 14/2/1941	ARP Motor Despatch Rider

Appendix Two
Birmingham Air Raids

Date	Action	Dead	Injured
25th/26 June 1940	First serious air raid on Birmingham		
14th July 1940	Luftwaffe reconnaissance of Birmingham		
9th August 1940	Early am raid	11	20
13th August 1940	Three and a half hour raid on Birmingham	7	20
15th August 1940	Three hour raid on Stechford area	11	13
17th August 1940	Three hour raid		
24th August 1940	Luftwaffe launch massive attack to cripple RAF	25	
26th/27th August 1940	Major raid on Sparkhill, Balsall Heath & Small Heath	3	10
27th/28th August 1940	Major raid on Sparkhill, Balsall Heath & Small Heath		
28th/29th August 1940	Major raid on Sparkhill, Balsall Heath & Small Heath		
30th/31st August 1940	Major raid on Sparkhill, Balsall Heath & Small Heath		
31st Aug/1st Sept 1940	Major raid on Sparkhill, Balsall Heath & Small Heath		
2nd September 1940	109 incidents reported		
23rd September 1940	Luftwaffe reconnaissance off Birmingham		
27th September 1940	Fort Dunlop daylight attack		
15th/16th October 1940	Heavy raid on Birmingham, start of weeks of raids	59	
16th October	Bomb on Bishop Street		
24th/25th October 1940	Major raid on city centre and area south of New Street Station, seven hours.		
25th/26th October 1940	Raid on Holloway Head, Constitution Hill. A wall of fire from Show Hill to the Council House	19	
26th/27th October 1940	Bomb explodes in front of screen at Carlton cinema Sparkbrook		
31st October 1940	Raid		
12th November 1940	Curzon St bombed		
13th November 1940	Daylight raid on Austin Works		
18th/19th November 1940	Raid lasting nine hours and forty minutes: BSA Works badly damaged.	53	

Date	Action	Dead	Injured
22nd/23rd November 1940	Worst raid on Birmingham, three water mains destroyed, much of the city without water		
27th November 1940	600 fires started, the BSA is hit again		
3rd December 1940	Four and a half hour raid, Bordesley Green and Aston		
10th December 1940	13,705 children evacuated from Birmingham		
11th/12th December 1940	Very Severe raid on Birmingham, thirteen and a half hours	104	
13th December 1940	Raid		
1st January 1941	Land mine in Alfred Street, Stoney Lane area		12
11th March 1941	Severe attack on Erdington		12
7th April 1941	Raid Incendiaries dropped		
9th April 1941	Two bombs dropped on Grange Road, Small Heath	3	
10th April 1941	Raids on Digbeth, Nechells, Small Heath	Many Killed	
9th May 1941	Garrison Lane bombed		
16th May 1941	Raid on Aston		
4th June 1941	A few bombs dropped		
12th August 1941	A few bombs dropped		
13th August 1941	Bombs dropped on burning factories		
4th July 1941	Minor raid		
28th June 1942	Raid for one and a half hours		
23rd July 1942	Air raid alert		
27th July 1942	Lone aircraft fails in attempt to bomb Saltley Gas Works		
28th July 1942	Raids on south west of the City, some 263 fires started		
31st July 1942	Raid, 41 fires reported		
23rd April 1943	Two bombs fell on Bordesley Green		
12th September 1944	Birmingham Fire Guard of 50,000 volunteers stood down		
13th December 1944	Home Guard disbanded		

While the above list deals with all the enemy action over Birmingham it is far from definitive in terms of the number of casualties and the level of damage inflicted on the City.

Index